OKANAGAN UNIVERSITY COLLEGE LIBRARY

D0448471

After the Holocaust

Erna F. Rubinstein is the author of
*The Survivor in Us All: Four Young Sisters
in the Holocaust* (Archon Books, 1983, 1986),
the prequel to this book. In both books
the events are true, but names have been changed
to protect the privacy of the individuals.

OKANAGAN UNIVERSITY COLLEGE
LIBRARY
BRITISH COLUMBIA

After the Holocaust

The Long Road to Freedom

Erna F. Rubinstein

Archon Books
1995

© 1995 Erna F. Rubinstein. All rights reserved.

First published 1995 as an Archon Book,
an imprint of The Shoe String Press, Inc.,
North Haven, Connecticut 06473.

Library of Congress Cataloging-in-Publication Data

Rubinstein, Erna F.
    After the Holocaust: the long road to freedom /
Erna F. Rubinstein.
        p.   cm.
    Summary: Having survived Auschwitz,
the author and her three sisters try
to begin life anew in wartorn Europe.
    ISBN 0-208-02421-2 (alk. paper)
    1. Rubinstein, Erna F.   2. Jews—Germany—Biography.
3. Holocaust survivors—Germany—Biography.
[1. Rubinstein, Erna F.   2. Jews—Biography.
3. Holocaust survivors.]   I. Title.
DS135.G5R837   1995
943'.004924'0092—dc20
[B]   95–21102
                                                                    CIP
                                                                     AC

The paper used in this publication
meets the minimum requirements of
American National Standard for Information Sciences—
Permanence of Paper for Printed Library Materials,
ANSI Z39.48–1984 ♾

Printed in the United States of America

This book is dedicated to my two wonderful children, Vivian Ann and Jeffrey Dan, and their loving families.

I wish also to express my gratitude to Kezia Raffel Pride for editing this manuscript, and to Susan Negelson for her help in rewriting it.

E.F.R.

Contents

Contents

Part Three
Many Roads to Freedom

Part Four
Free at Last

Foreword

How often one hears that the Holocaust ended in 1945. It is true that the military war ended then. But for survivors of the *Shoah*, the aftermath was another form of survival. The psychic wounds, the nightmares, the wrenching memories of lost families, friends, and communities would not, could not, and should not, go away. Survivors—and there were not many of them—had lived through an unprecedented attempt to annihilate Judaism and the Jewish people. Abandoned to their fate during the war, put in "displaced persons" camps—frequently along with their former tormentors—afterwards, the survivors had to decide whether to turn their backs on society or attempt to improve the world.

Erna Rubinstein, an Auschwitz survivor, has written a book that tells the tale of one woman's determination to help transform her experience into a lesson. With great skill, intelligence, and passion in the person of "Ruth" she tells of her own survival and, miraculously, that of her three sisters, and the deaths of her parents and brother. Erna's story is gripping. Following her liberation, she worked with refugees; helping those whom no one wanted. She pulls no punches in describing the antisemitism that was directed against her *after* the Holocaust, even by some she attempted to help. Yet, her book also tells the story of one woman's enormous energy and coping skills. These enabled her to embrace life.

Her readers will learn several important things about survivors from Erna Rubinstein. First, the importance of choosing life. She writes movingly about her post-*Shoah* marriage, her family, and her pursuit of higher education.

Second, hatred is not the answer to the Holocaust. Indeed, there is no answer. Rather, teaching and helping others to understand must be the post-Holocaust goal. Third, Erna describes her continuing faith in God, both during and after the *Shoah*. Her response underscores the complexity of faith after Auschwitz. Finally, in a world that permits genocide, allows children to starve, and grows increasingly chaotic, both morally and politically, Erna Rubinstein issues a challenge to us all. We can and must do better.

Prof. Alan L. Berger
Raddock Chair of Holocaust Studies
Florida Atlantic University

Part One
First Steps Out of Darkness

1. *"The Americans Are Coming!"*

"The Americans are coming, the Americans are coming!" The echo sounded all across the mountain, like a ghostly prayer.

The war had lasted so many years. I remember the day it started: September 1, 1939. I was seventeen years old. My father loaded the whole family on a wagon and we headed east, away from the German border, away from the battle-front. My father sat proudly in the wagon; he was taking his family to safety. Mother loaded all the food she could find into the wagon; it would be enough to feed us for a few days, until the Polish Army repelled the Germans and we could return safely home.

I sat in the wagon with my three younger sisters and my eight-year-old brother, whom we all adored. This picture will forever stay in my heart, for this was the last time we were all together.

It took the Germans just three weeks to occupy all of Poland. They immediately began to carry out the war on the Jews. In the beginning they moved all the Jewish people into ghettos. We were surrounded by a wall, separated from the Polish population. While living in the ghettos, we had to perform very hard labor for stingy rations. Many were shot, often with no provocation whatsoever, simply because they were Jewish. Little children who couldn't work for the Germans were summarily executed, usually with their mothers.

From the ghettos we were moved into concentration camps, where we had to do hard physical labor with only starvation rations. Anyone who couldn't produce up to the Germans' standards was shot instantly. On a daily basis, we

3

were all paraded before the camp commandants, who decided based on a quick visual survey who was fit to live and who was sick and therefore should die. Those segregated out in this manner were shipped away to extermination camps such as Auschwitz, never to be seen again. Millions of innocent people were killed.

In the last days of April 1945, the Germans realized that the end of the Third Reich was imminent. The Allies were advancing, and the fall of the German Army was inevitable. They herded together as many concentration camp inmates as they could and marched us away from the camps. They didn't want the Americans and British to find evidence of the extermination and the atrocities they had committed. Most of the camp inmates, however, were unable to walk, so the SS, the *Schutzstaffel*, Hitler's elite guard unit, shot them, or else left them in the camps to die of starvation or disease. When the liberating armies reached the camps, the stench was so terrible that the soldiers could not enter.

The "death march," as we called it, was appropriately named, for not many survived it. Those of us who had managed to walk out of the camps were not in much better shape than those who had been left behind. We marched through the German countryside, surrounded by the SS; when someone succumbed to starvation and exhaustion and could walk no further, the SS guards were always at the ready with their machine guns.

After years of torture, starvation, and hard labor, those of us who had survived this long knew that if we were to live, we had to make this final effort. We couldn't comprehend how the farmers along our route could watch us die of starvation; nobody, but nobody, would reach out to us with a slice of bread or a drop of milk. Every day more and more of the women in our group could no longer walk; when they couldn't even stand, they were loaded onto a wagon to be buried during the night, either dead or still alive, in the dark forests of Germany.

The death march seemed never-ending, continuing for many days and nights. We received no food, no water, and almost no rest. We marched and marched in those last days of winter, often trudging through snow. We were dressed in our thin blue and white uniforms, no underwear, many of us with no shoes, nothing to protect us from the elements. When we were allowed to rest through the night, our only choice was to lie down in the snow. We often awoke surprised to be alive.

One day as we trudged through a small village, an older woman sidled up and whispered to one of the girls that the war would be over soon. The Americans were coming, she said. "The Americans are coming!" The rumor spread quickly through all the rows of marching women. We wanted so much to believe it. It gave us hope that we would survive this deadly march, the hunger, the pain, the cold. Perhaps we'd really live to see the end of the war.

One night we reached a large barn far up in the mountains, somewhere between Germany and German-occupied Czechoslovakia. It seemed like the end of the world. There was nothing in sight but fields and woods. There wasn't a human being around; only the barely breathing wrecks of hundreds of women, surrounded by SS guards, machine guns poised on their shoulders, always ready. In the morning, when the sun's rays came slanting through the holes in the barn, there appeared hundreds of helpless shadows lying on the dusty floor.

I tried to get up, but couldn't. My body wouldn't move. My eyes wandered, looking for my sisters. I saw Anna and Mania getting up; Pola couldn't move. Starvation had finally triumphed.

I prayed to God, as I always did, and a miracle happened. A woman sitting next to me handed me a few kernels of wheat which she had found beneath the floor of the barn. I gave a few to Pola and swallowed a few myself. Suddenly Pola pointed to a hole under the barn. It was a very small opening, and at first I couldn't imagine that anyone could squeeze inside it. But we could walk no further, and I realized our only hope to escape these tortures lay in hiding.

Five of us squeezed in one by one, with hardly any room

to move. Another woman covered the hole with straw, so we wouldn't be visible. We huddled together, waiting for the moment of truth. The SS guards chased everybody out of the barn. Then they conducted their search to see if anyone was hiding, trying to remain behind. We held our breath. The straw above us moved, and the barrel of a machine gun poked through. It was over. A guard had found us—but, incredibly, he left! He hadn't seen us! Maybe he couldn't imagine that anyone—even a stick person—could get through such a tiny opening.

The death march moved on without us. We huddled in our den for hours, afraid to come out. Finally, when it grew dark again, we emerged. We were hardly able to walk, but somehow we managed to reach a dark forest, where we decided to lie down for the night. The morning sun awakened us.

My youngest sister, Anna, was the first one to stretch out and to greet us with a smile. She was only nine years old when the war started. I remembered when her head was covered with long, black hair; now, at fifteen, she was bald like the rest of us, our hair shaved in Auschwitz to be used for stuffing German mattresses. There was no room for children in the concentration camps, and Anna always had to try to look older, to keep her head high and her back straight, and her eyes wide open at all times. She was bright and somehow learned to face danger, despite her young age. She was, with the help of a few miracles, able to endure the horrors of Auschwitz.

Pola was the next. At seventeen, she looked fragile, but she was very beautiful, despite her bald head, which had once been covered with magnificent blond hair. Mother used to always say how quick-thinking she was. Pola would get into trouble, but would get out of it just as fast. For Pola, the end of the war had come not a moment too soon; she had reached the end of her endurance. Mother was right: It was Pola who had spotted the hole under the barn and saved us all.

My sister Mania was a year younger than I. It was she who believed that we would survive, no matter what. Her smile was soft and her manner calm and controlled. She could survive on very little food, or so it seemed, for she always shared her meager rations with us, helping us to avoid starvation. In the world of the camps one bite of bread could save a life, and indeed it did at times. Some evenings, before we lay our exhausted bodies to sleep, Mania wanted to talk to us about our parents and our little brother, Moshe. She had dreams that they were alive somewhere, somehow.

As for myself, I was twenty-three years old, but I looked and felt like an old woman. My head was completely bald, my body nothing but skin and bones, my arms and legs shaking with cold and malnutrition. My blue eyes were wild with fear, staring into the unknown darkness. I had to wonder whether it was really me. Could it be me? Could it be the same girl who had graduated from high school only six years before and had great plans for her future? I was already promised a job as a secretary to the director of one of the largest paper mills in Poland. I was surrounded by a wonderful, loving family. I had hopes and dreams. My family lived in a small village in the mountains. In the summer we all went mountain climbing, and in the winter we went skiing. We lived a full and happy life. And now?

Moshe, our eleven-year-old brother, was dead. Our father had hidden him in the concentration camp, Plaszow, for as long as he could. When the Germans discovered that there were children hidden in the camp, they threw them on the trucks and took them to Auschwitz. When they arrived there, the children were taken to the showers, but instead of water, gas came down. The 360 little children, my brother Moshe among them, died in the gas chambers of Auschwitz.

Father had been shipped from one concentration camp to another until he arrived in Mauthausen. We did not know what had happened to him. Logic told us he must be dead, but we all hoped and prayed we would find him alive.

Mother had arrived with us in Auschwitz after a horrifying journey in cattle trains, and she hoped that we could all stay together and help each other survive. But there was a segregation soon after we came—the Nazis separated out those who would die right away—and before we realized what was happening, she was pushed away from us. That same night, we watched the fire burning. In it was the body of our beloved mother. She was only forty-three years old.

Still, I was lucky; I had my sisters with me. It was hard to believe that the four of us had survived the Holocaust together. Hitler's aim was to break the Jewish family. There were no families untouched, none who didn't lose loved ones. For four sisters to survive was really a miracle. It was a miracle we manufactured for ourselves, however; it took a lot of work, and constant alertness. We never reported as sisters. We changed our names and ages many times, and always tried to stay separate, yet together, so we would be assigned to the same camp. In Auschwitz, as we stood to be numbered, I made sure that a friend or relative stood between each of us. Many years later I went to Australia, and found an aunt who had survived the war (though she lost her husband—my mother's brother—and a seven-year-old son). She showed me her number, which was exactly next to mine. "Don't you remember?" she asked. I shook my head, and she explained that I had asked her to stand between me and my youngest sister, Anna, so the camp guards would not connect us as family. That could have meant instant death. Besides, if anything happened to me, she would take care of Anna.

No matter what critical circumstances we were in, we had to be aware of each other. When we had to perform unbelievably hard labor, I would always be there for my youngest sister to help her carry the heavy load. We shared our last piece of bread or drop of soup with whichever one couldn't take the hunger anymore. We were always together, praying together, helping each other, often risking our own lives to assure each other's survival.

Mania, Pola, and Anna were my real sisters, but I also had another sister. Gienia had been on the death march with us. When people couldn't walk anymore, the SS guards would push them onto a wagon and during the night we had to dig a hole somewhere in the forest and bury them, whether they were dead or alive. One day I saw Gienia on the wagon.

I didn't even stop to think for a moment, but rushed over and pulled her off, risking my own life. My sisters and I almost carried her for the rest of the day, for she could barely stay upright. She was tall and emaciated, a walking skeleton. Her eyes were huge, and her head bald. It was frightening to look at her; to me she looked like she was a breath away from death.

The night we hid under the barn, we pulled Gienia in with us, for she had become our sister. When we left the barn the next night, we literally had to carry her through the woods, until finally we too lost our strength. Only after we reached a stream and drank some water were we able to crawl again. When we stretched our bodies out on the forest floor that night, we were afraid that Gienia would not wake up the next morning.

But when we were awakened by the morning sun, all of us, including Gienia, opened our eyes. It took us a little time to realize where we were; we had slept under open skies, no guns pointing at us, and no SS guards pushing us around. Lo and behold, there were no electric fences around us. We touched each other; we looked into each other's eyes, held hands, and slowly stood up.

"We are alive! We are free!" we screamed with all our might.

"We made it!" Mania shouted, "Didn't I tell you we would make it?" She sounded so happy, for the first time in six years. We all wanted to rejoice, we wanted to run, but we barely had the strength to move.

"Let's follow the sun," Anna yelled.

We looked at her, and as she started rolling down the hill, we all followed. We followed the sun, and suddenly the forest ended; we had reached the bottom of the hill. As we looked around we could see some houses, and hope awakened in us. Perhaps somebody would share a little food with us, anything to eat; we were literally starving to death.

We walked slowly, scared that someone might be following us. Suddenly Pola grabbed me and pointed me in one direction. I turned around and saw a strange-looking vehicle.

As we came closer, we could see several soldiers standing around it. We were terribly frightened and held tightly to each other. We wanted to run, but we were stuck to the ground. The soldiers came closer to us, waving and pointing at themselves, saying: "American, American." We knew they were trying to tell us something, but we were so very scared. Could they really be Americans? What if they were pretending? Who knew what they could do to us? We wanted to trust them; we hoped they really were Americans. For so many years we had been hoping and praying for the Americans to come and save us.

We all stood motionless as the soldiers advanced, smiling. I'll never forget the look on their faces when they got close enough to see us. They were still smiling, but at the same time they looked startled, for we didn't look human. Our bulging eyes, bald heads, and cadaverous bodies, covered with blue and white striped uniforms, were like nothing they had ever seen before. Their penetrating stares frightened us.

"They will report us to the Germans," Anna gasped.

"We'll all be killed for running away from the death march," Gienia added, panic in her voice.

We had to escape again. We couldn't trust anyone. We didn't want to be followed, so we headed toward the deep forest, moving as fast as our feeble bodies could go. Once in the forest, we looked for berries, anything to swallow, but there was nothing. We were so hungry and so weak.

It was almost dark when we reached a village. We knocked at the first door, and a woman let us in. She offered us some leftovers from her dinner, and volunteered the room where her husband had a cobbler's bench. There were no beds, but we could sleep on the floor. She told us that we were now in German-occupied Czechoslovakia. We weren't exactly sure where that was; all we knew was that we were thrilled to be out of Germany.

The woman's husband was still somewhere with the army. World War II had lasted much too long for these Czech families. The men were still somewhere in the mountains fighting, or just trying to end the war. The women and children were waiting for them anxiously. In the meantime, another strange army had come into the village. The Czechs soon learned that it was the Americans, and all the inhabitants came out to greet their liberators. "The war is over, the war is over," they heard the soldiers explain. But they didn't believe them, for the planes were roaring above, and their men had not returned home.

The woman who gave us shelter had a little boy, who held onto her skirt, and her big belly showed that she was expecting another baby any day. She handed us some potatoes, which we devoured, and as soon as we stretched out on the floor we were all asleep. The sun was shining as we opened our eyes and awakened to spring. The air was warm, but our bodies cold. We had been starving for such a long time, we didn't have an ounce of body fat to keep us warm. We shivered from hunger and cold.

We heard noises outside the house, and rushed into the courtyard. There was a crowd gathering around a vehicle, just like the one we had seen the day before. The villagers pointed at the soldiers, who were saying, "Americans, Americans." The people surrounded the vehicle and the soldiers handed them some canned food. "Hitler *kaput*, Germany *kaput*," we heard them say. We thought that we understood what they were trying to tell us, but we simply couldn't comprehend what was happening. Our eyes filled with tears. We stood wondering: Does this mean that the Germans can't hurt us anymore? Can it be true, that we are free? Where can we go? Can we go back home, to Poland, where we lived before the war? Can we return to our parents? How can we live without them? What are we to do?

The birds were flying above, the sun was shining, the trees were green, the flowers in bloom. There was music in the air. World War II had ended. I felt like screaming and yelling and shouting: "I'm free! I'm alive!" All I could think about was that the world was free now, that there would be no wars anymore. The words of the prophet Isaiah had finally come true: "And they shall beat their swords into plowshares, and their spears into pruning hooks; nation shall

11

not lift up sword against nation, neither shall they learn war any more." My world would be free: free of wars, free of persecution.

"The war is over! You are free!" the soldiers shouted.

"The war is over!" repeated the Czech women around them.

I felt a tremendous trembling in my body; a sudden desire to join in on this celebration overcame me. I pulled my sisters together, and we all yelled, "The war is over!" hoping that the whole world could hear us.

The echo carried through the mountains and we all sighed with relief. The long war is over . . .

2. "Germany Kaput!"

It was May 1945. Spring was in the air, yet nothing seemed real. The five of us were alive, but we were in a small village somewhere in Czechoslovakia. The people around us spoke a strange language. We could understand some of it, because it was similar to Polish, but the people here looked at us as if we were creatures from another dimension. Our bald heads and odds and ends of clothes made them wonder about us. They were running, rushing, screaming; we couldn't understand the meaning of it all. Were they afraid of the Americans? Should we be? After all these years of dreaming, hoping and praying that the Americans would come end the war and our suffering, should we be afraid now? Why couldn't we just relax, start making plans for our future, and enjoy being free?

For days we sat in the little workroom that had been offered us, afraid to go out in our blue and white striped uniforms. The Americans had given us a couple of blankets, and with these we made skirts. Mania was very good at sewing, and she also made blouses from the sheets that our hostess had given us. Finally one morning, all dressed up in our bedroom finery, we decided to go over to where the American army was stationed. We had to find out for ourselves what was really happening, and whether the Americans could help us.

Everywhere we looked, we saw men in uniform. Officers, soldiers; we looked at their faces, not much older than ours, and we couldn't wait to tell them how grateful we were that they had come to save us. We wanted to tell them how glad we were to see their khaki uniforms, instead of the green ones the German army wore, but we couldn't find the words, or the courage to speak. We were frightened of everything; we didn't know who to trust.

Before the war, I had studied English at school and could speak fluently; but all through the years in concentration camps, I was afraid even to think in English for fear the Germans would kill me as a spy. I had to erase all knowledge of English from my brain. Now, when I needed it, I couldn't find it.

When we finally worked up our courage, we walked over to where the men were standing. We shook hands with the soldiers and innocently threw them kisses, and they responded by handing us more blankets and some cans of food. Little did we know that the soldiers too were overjoyed with the end of the war, and having been away from home and from their loved ones for such a long time, they too were hungry for affection. Odd-looking as we may have been, we were still five young girls. That night the men came for us.

Mila, our pregnant hostess, was sleeping in the main room of the house with her four-year-old son. My sisters and I were asleep in the workshop, at the other end of the house. In the middle of the night, I was awakened by a knock on the door. I shuddered when I heard it, and it took me a moment to realize where I was. Knocks were always frightening to us, for the Germans politely knocked on the door when they came to take people to be killed. My sisters were also awake now, and they were petrified. They huddled in the corner and their eyes begged me not to open the door.

"Be quiet and stay where you are," I whispered. My heart was pounding wildly as I opened the door to the workshop. I opened it just a crack, only enough to see who it was. There before me stood a giant man in a khaki uniform. He tried to push his way inside the room, but I moved in front of him and closed the door behind me. I was shaking. I desperately searched my mind, looking for the words I had put there long, long ago. Suddenly my mouth opened, and I heard myself uttering: "My children sleeping." I was shocked by the words. But I knew that I could not let this man hurt us. My sisters had become my children; I had to protect them from any more harm. It was my job now that my parents were no longer here to take care of them.

The officer in front of me saluted, and said in a drunken slur: "Children . . . I'm sorry," and he started to walk away. I was wracked with fear, and my heart pumped so hard I thought it would leap out of my chest, but suddenly I realized that I was now in a different place in time. I understood that this man, drunk or not, had emotions. This man had respect for children. He had feelings. He was *human*. In the world I had been living in for six long years, the children were the first to be killed. Over a million children were wiped off the face of the earth and nobody cared. The men who watched them burn didn't have any feelings; they didn't shed any tears; they didn't feel for those children and their parents, even though they themselves had children at home. The man who stood before me now had feelings. He was drunk with alcohol and the end of the war, but he had emotions, and when I said that my children were sleeping, he walked away.

With relief I went back into the house and comforted my sisters, telling them that someone had knocked by mistake. "Everything is all right," I soothed. "Try to go back to sleep."

Suddenly, we heard a scream from the kitchen: *"Holki, holki, wlazl na mnie!*—Girls, girls, he climbed on top of me!" I rushed into the kitchen as a young, drunken soldier was running out. Mila tried to explain to me what had happened, but I only understood half of it. All I knew was that he wanted to rape her, but when she started screaming, he realized that there must be someone else in the house, and he ran away. My heart sank; I was furious and frightened at the same time. I walked over to Mila and touched her face. I gently rubbed her belly, trying to assure her that the baby inside would be all right. She was crying, and I didn't know what to say. How could I explain this American soldier to her?

Americans. They were our liberators; we prayed for

them, we blessed them. How could they do this to her? What would happen to her baby? Mila sat shaking, frightened for her baby, and I was terrified for all of us. I looked over at my sisters, who were standing in the doorway of the kitchen. The looks on their faces told the whole story. Fear! "Is this our future?" their faces said. "Will we forever be afraid? What should we believe in now? How can we go on living? Have we come this far, through this much, only to find that there is no one we can trust, no one we can turn to for help?"

I stumbled back to our room, locking the door, and found three of my sisters ready to run. They were trying to get Mania to come, but she was on the floor motionless. She was unable to move, unable to speak. She was curled up on the floor, her eyes full of blank terror. We all gathered around her, cuddling her and speaking softly to her. We spent the rest of the night trying to figure out what to do. The light of the new day brought with it a decision. We had to leave this border village before something else happened. With our words of comfort and encouragement, Mania slowly began to move and her speech returned, but we were all frightened and worried about her.

We were sad to leave Mila, who was the first person in the world to help us and give us shelter, but we knew that we couldn't stay. This was not home for us. We had to find a place where we could feel safe. We left the village and walked for hours until we reached a small town called Susice. There were soldiers everywhere. They stared at us, and again we felt lost and terribly alone.

As we were walking through the town, we were approached by two young soldiers, who asked us in broken German whether we were Jewish. The question frightened us. Should we answer? What would happen to us if we answered yes? They saw our fear, and tried to calm us. Finally, we nodded in response. The soldiers started talking to us, but we couldn't understand what they were trying to say. They motioned for us to follow them, and in a few minutes we arrived at a city building where the American army was stationed.

We walked inside and the soldiers called out to a young man in uniform. He turned when he heard his name. His hair was neatly cut, his jaw clean-shaven. His eyes shone as he looked at us. He shook hands with each one of us and then pointed at himself: "Rabbi, *rebbe.*" We just stared at him. What would a rabbi be doing in uniform? The way we remembered rabbis at home, in Poland, they wore long, black coats, and had *peyos* (sidecurls) and beards, and they certainly wouldn't shake hands with women—that was forbidden by purity laws. How could this man before us be a rabbi? I turned to look at my sisters and said, "How will we ever understand these Americans?"

The young rabbi, whose name was Eugene Lipman, motioned for us to join him around the table. In minutes a few soldiers appeared carrying bowls of food, the kind of food we had been dreaming about for six years. There was spaghetti and meatballs, noodle soup, and bread, lots of bread. We could not remember the last time we had seen so much food. Our eyes were wide with astonishment and hunger.

The rabbi whispered something with his head down and his eyes closed. It sounded like a prayer to us, so we put our heads down, but before he had even finished we grabbed the food and started to devour it. We kept looking at each other. We couldn't believe that all this food was ours to eat, to savor, to enjoy. Pola held up a piece of bread and said to me, "Can I eat the whole slice?" She was so used to having to ration each bite, to share each paltry piece of food with her sisters, that she couldn't fathom a whole piece of bread all to herself. I told her she could eat all she wanted, but then I cautioned my sisters to be careful. "Remember what happened when we found a potato and ate it, and it almost cost us our lives." We had been so long without food that we could no longer digest normally. After we had eaten the potato we got diarrhea. We were lucky, however, because we did not become dehydrated like so many others who survived long years of torture in the concentration camps, only to die when they ate their first meal. I urged my sisters to eat

17

slowly. They stopped only when the rabbi assured us that we could take all of the leftover food home.

Home? Didn't he understand that we had no home? I tried to explain, but he couldn't understand. Anna turned to him and whispered, "We are free?"

He opened his arms wide. "You are free! Hitler *kaput*, Germany *kaput*. Americans are here. You can go home."

"Go home?" Pola asked, "Where is our home?" We all looked at each other and then back at the rabbi. We used our hands, broken English, and German, trying desperately to make him understand. "We have no home. We have no place to go."

Finally his face showed us that he understood. He told us to stay there and wait for him, and he ran out the door. We could only hope that he would be able to find a home for us. We waited what seemed like hours. Finally he returned with two other officers. He motioned for us to get in his jeep. We drove into town. Where was he taking us? My sisters and I kept looking at each other. The rabbi stopped at a large city building and told us to stay in the jeep. When he came back out, he wore a big grin. He was holding a key. He started the jeep, and we rode in complete silence to the edge of town. We were still in Susice, a Czech town occupied by the Germans during the war, and slowly beginning to recover under the American occupation.

The jeep stopped in front of a nice, big house. The rabbi tried his best to explain to us that the Germans who had occupied this house had escaped before the Americans came to town. We finally understood that the house was empty, and for now it was ours to live in. The rabbi opened the front door, and we walked into the house. I looked over at my sisters and put my arms around them. We were all laughing. We were so excited; we could hardly believe our good fortune. This was the first time we had been in a real house since September 1939, when we left our family home in Poland.

We ran from room to room. This was a real home. There was a kitchen, and even a bathroom. We touched each and every piece of furniture. There were beds—not wooden boards, but real beds with warm blankets and clean sheets. The rabbi watched us with amazement and joy. We were like little babies discovering life.

And yet, we were still afraid. What if the soldiers came again during the night? How could we keep them from walking into our home? Between the five of us we managed to tell the rabbi what had happened to us at Mila's house, and we tried to explain our fears to him. He understood our concern, and before we went to sleep there was a twenty-four-hour guard posted outside the house.

Rabbi Lipman left, and we yelled and screamed. We still couldn't believe that we had a home. We drew lots to see who would sleep where. We found food in the kitchen, but we were afraid to eat it, for the Germans had left it behind and we thought it might be poisoned. We searched every corner of the house for fear that someone was hiding there. Finally, when we were satisfied that we were safe, we locked the doors and crawled into bed. We were completely and utterly exhausted.

I lay in a bed for the first time in six years; I was exhausted beyond imagination, and yet I couldn't sleep. I saw a full moon through the window, and suddenly I thought I saw God. My body and mind were overwhelmed by the sight. I could feel it. I could almost touch it. I tried to find the words of prayer, but I couldn't. I was overpowered by a wonderful feeling of peace, a feeling of tranquillity I had never experienced before. I closed my eyes and fell asleep, hoping that this dream would never end.

3. "I Have a Job for You . . ."

The sun was shining, but I felt chilly when I awoke the next morning. The two American soldiers were watching our house, and for a moment I thought of going outside to try to talk to them. I wanted to ask them some questions; I wanted them to tell me about freedom and the war being over, but I had an overwhelming urge to check on my sisters. I opened each door fearful that their beds would be empty, but I found them all sleeping.

I wandered through the house touching pieces of furniture, trying to convince myself that the war was over and life could continue again. I went from room to room just looking and touching. The last door I opened led to the bathroom. My eyes scanned the room and there to my astonishment was the most fantastic thing—a bathtub! I could barely remember what a bathtub looked like, much less the possible enjoyment and pleasure it would provide. I quickly walked over to the tub; I knew exactly what I wanted to do. I hadn't experienced such luxury for a long time.

I filled the tub and stepped in slowly. When the hot water caressed me, I began to run my hands over my body. There was hardly any flesh on me; all I could feel was bones. I closed my eyes, and in my mind's eye I saw only a skeleton. My head, completely shaved at Auschwitz, was just slightly covered with light blond hair. I touched my breasts and found only two small raisins sticking out. I had a difficult time recognizing my body, even though I could feel it, I could touch it. It seemed like the body of a stranger. My recollection was from a long time ago, and I remembered my

20

body full and rounded, though not fat, my head covered with long blond hair.

Suddenly, the door flew open, and my sisters came running into the bathroom.

"A bathtub!" Pola squealed happily. "I'm dying to take a bath."

"Oh, it looks so heavenly," Anna chimed in.

"All right," I said, "give me five minutes and then it's all yours."

I shooed them out of the room, and then I stood up to get out of the tub. That's when I saw the mirror. It seemed like hundreds of years since I'd seen myself in a mirror—the last time I could recall was six years ago. I had a date. I was seventeen and he was twenty. I had to look good, and perhaps even more, mature. I combed my hair this way and that way. I put on a little lipstick, which I usually didn't use. I wore the best dress I could find, and I thought I looked pretty good. He thought so, too. But that was another time, another life.

I walked slowly over to the mirror until my reflection came into view. I was shocked. I looked at a small child staring back at me. My eyes stood out, but even they looked strange to me. They looked bluish, greenish—I couldn't tell. This was, indeed, the body of a stranger!

A new day was beginning for me. I knew I had to do something. I had to reach out for this new life; a life of freedom and a life of peace. I had to begin somewhere, but where and how I didn't quite know.

During the day a young soldier arrived with food supplies and bundles of army shirts and uniforms; he also brought parachutes. He explained very slowly that the army chaplain, Rabbi Lipman, had sent him. He apologized for not speaking German or Polish. I opened my mouth to respond, and started speaking to him in clear English. He was shocked, but no more than I, since I had not heard or spoken English for six years. I felt as if my brain had opened up and words that were hidden there came rushing out. A deadened part of

21

me had come back to life, and it gave me hope. I thanked the soldier with all my heart, because we could certainly use the food, and we could sew the clothes to fit us and make scarves to cover our bald heads. These gifts made us feel more human than we had in years.

We still had a difficult time walking the streets of this town, Susice, because even though it was in Czechoslovakia, it had been occupied for years by the Germans. Since it was so close to the German border, many Germans had moved there. The fear of being surrounded by our enemy hardly ever left us. Fortunately, there was a tremendous number of American army men stationed in Susice, and their presence was somewhat reassuring.

One Sunday morning, the last week in May, Rabbi Lipman held services for all the armed forces in the area. It was to be a thanksgiving service for victory and the end of the war. The rabbi asked me if I would like to attend. I was still frightened to be among thousands of soldiers, but my sisters urged me to go, and so I agreed. Rabbi Lipman picked me up in his jeep, and when we arrived at the auditorium he showed me to a seat in front of him. He knew that I was scared, and he held my hand until it was time to start the service. He began by reciting a Hebrew blessing that was familiar to me. I was surprised to hear him speak Hebrew to this tremendous crowd of soldiers, all of different faiths and from different walks of life.

As the rabbi continued in English, I was able to pick out some words. He kept repeating the word "peas." I was surprised, because the only "peas" I could think of were the green peas I had once upon a time picked in my grandmother's garden. Those peas always tasted so sweet, and my stomach ached for them. I could almost feel them on my tongue. I couldn't for the life of me understand why an army chaplain would talk so much about peas to all these soldiers who had just fought such a fierce war.

When the service was over, the rabbi came over to me and asked me if I had understood what he was talking about. He wanted to know what I thought of his sermon.

"Good, good," I uttered. "But why did you talk so much about peas?"

"Peace . . . oh, peas," he whispered.

He took me to his jeep and drove to the officers' mess. He went into the kitchen and soon returned with a big bowl of sweet green peas. I couldn't believe my eyes. He understood what I had been dreaming about for so many years.

"Yes, peas, peas," I blurted out as I started to devour them.

The rabbi watched me anxiously, and when I was almost finished cleaning the bowl, he asked me, "Were those the peas you thought I was talking about?"

"Yes, yes," I nodded enthusiastically.

The rabbi took my hand and patiently explained to me the "peace" he was talking about. He spoke about war and peace, about the American Army that had fought the war and finally won it, with the loss of so many lives. He tried to tell me that I didn't need to be afraid of the Germans anymore. There was peace on earth, he repeated again and again. I felt like crying and laughing at the same time. I listened to every word he said, and tried to instill the word "peace" in my mind and in my heart.

When Rabbi Lipman took me home, he carried another big bowl of peas for my sisters.

We all stayed inside the house most of the time. Mania tried to scrape together fabric to sew clothes for us. She would make blouses out of sheets, and skirts from the army parachutes—anything to replace the concentration camp uniforms. For the better part of the day, we would just sit on the floor, talking. Mania would talk of staying in this big house forever. Pola and Anna would disagree, saying this was not our home and we did not belong here. The debate went on and on, until sometimes Pola and Anna would get so upset that they would run to their rooms and stay there for hours.

We were petrified to go out. All the years of suffering and imprisonment kept us in constant fear. We feared the

Germans! This was a difficult thing to shake. I wasn't sure that we would ever be able to feel safe again. The next time I saw the chaplain, I tried to explain it to him, but he just couldn't understand. I kept telling him how frightened we were to stay in this town, surrounded by Germans— Germans, who could incinerate us at any time, just as they had done to our parents, our brother Moshe, and most of our relatives and friends. I struggled to explain our fears.

Rabbi Lipman tried to convince me that I was wrong. "Can't you see that the American Army is here to protect you? The war is over, Germany *kaput*," he kept repeating, but it just didn't register. I could not trust it. I worried constantly. I worried for my sisters; I just couldn't stop worrying. That night after the rabbi left, I tried to figure out how we could get away. I believed that we would never be safe in Susice; we had to get as far away from the German border as we could.

The next morning I woke up early, hearing voices from Anna's room. I rushed in and Pola was sitting on her bed, crying. "I'm sick," Anna whispered. I touched her forehead; she was burning up with fever. I gave her some water to drink and then I rushed over to the officers' quarters, looking desperately for the rabbi. He told me that there was no doctor around, but he did manage to get some aspirin and brought it over for Anna. Now I knew there was no way we could stay in this town. We had to go somewhere where Anna could get help.

I had heard from the Americans that the next town over was Prachatice, and that the American Army was stationed there. I begged the rabbi to help us get to Prachatice. A few hours later a truck was waiting in front of our house. We packed what few possessions we had and loaded them onto the truck. We put down blankets for Anna, and she lay on them, bright with fever. Within a couple of hours we were in Prachatice, and the driver brought us straight to the hospital. We had to wait a while, but eventually a nice Czech doctor came over and examined Anna. He gave her some medicine, and told us to go home.

Home? My God, what were we to do? We shared our fears with the driver. Again, he made some inquiries, and learned that there was an office for the American occupation forces in town. He took us there. I walked into the office, and started to speak to the admitting officer in clear English. The officer was amazed at my fluency. As he spoke to me, I was suddenly transported back to my high school English class.

I could see George standing in front of me. He was my English teacher. I was seventeen, going on eighteen, and I was madly in love with him. I studied day and night because I wanted so badly to please him and to get his attention. I even took private lessons from him; I just wanted to be close to him. Nothing happened between us, for as long as I was his student, he made sure of that. He certainly knew that I was in love with him; a blind man could have seen it. On the day I graduated from high school, I walked out with my diploma, and who should be waiting for me in front of the school building but George. But the war began, and we were separated. I often wondered what happened to him. It was many years later before I learned that the Nazis had killed him along with thousands of other professionals.

I forced my attention back to the officer in front of me. "Your English is very good," he announced. "I have a job for you. I could use an interpreter for the occupation forces. We have difficulty communicating with the Czechs. You do speak Czech, don't you?"

"I do understand Czech," I whispered, astonished and overjoyed at the offer. "Yes, yes, I would love a job," I blurted out. "But sir, we have no place to live, and my sister, she is sick, she needs a bed." I looked at him as if he was God. He had to help me.

I rushed outside to tell my sisters what had happened. In the meantime, the officer summoned the Czech mayor and ordered him to find proper living quarters for us.

The mayor drove us to the center of town. He stopped the jeep in front of a big house with a magnificent garden.

The house had belonged to a Jewish family who had not returned from the war. "This will be your house," he said.

We were stunned. We thanked our truck driver for bringing us here and kissed him gratefully. He unloaded our belongings and carried Anna inside the house. We put her in bed immediately. "We have a house; I have a bed," Anna whispered feverishly.

"We are home, can't you see?" Mania said happily.

"What are you talking about, what can we see?" Pola said, irritated, "This isn't our home."

We tiptoed through the house, afraid of ghosts. We looked at the photographs on the walls and discovered what the people in this house looked like before they were taken away. In one room, two small boys with brown eyes looked up at us from their picture frames. In another room, a little girl in a starched apron sat in a chair, smiling. The images of these children touched our hearts. Before I went to sleep that night I looked at the pictures again and the words of the Kaddish, the Jewish prayer for the dead, came to my lips: *Yitgadal veyitkadash shemey raba.* Magnified and sanctified be His great name . . .

There was no way I could sleep that night. The memory of my beloved mother and father, as well as my darling little brother Moshe, flowed into the vast pool of memory of these children and all the others, the million and a half children who were killed in Hitler's war against the Jews. I spent the night remembering.

We were four sisters, and we all wished we had a brother. When I was little, my mother told me that the stork brought babies. I would look for pictures of birds and find a stork. I would thank him for bringing my sisters into the world. One day a young woman who was helping my mother take care of us explained to me the whole process of having babies. I was amazed, but I never dared to ask Mother if it was true.

My poor mother, she was always so busy. She took care of the four of us, and also helped Father in the store. Some days, she would walk miles to a farm to get fresh vegetables. She always had to have fresh vegetables and fruits for us, which were not easy to get. There were no merchants who would bring fruit into our village in the winter. It was even difficult to store potatoes. We certainly didn't have refrigeration. The basement would stay cold enough to store potatoes, but fruit wouldn't last.

My mother always worried about her family. It wasn't just us she thought about, but also Grandmother and Grandfather, who lived on a farm about twenty-five kilometers (fifteen miles) from us, and her ten brothers and sisters. During the summer months we would hike to the farm in Sopotnia, and all through the winter we would go there on skis. The whole family came to our house on holidays. Mother cooked and cleaned for days. How did she ever do it all?

The year I celebrated my eleventh birthday, in the spring, I noticed that Mother was getting bigger. She had always been rather heavy, so I didn't think much of it. One evening, after serving dinner, Mother had just joined us at the table when she suddenly said quietly, "I think the baby is coming." We girls couldn't imagine what she was talking about. She got up from the table and went to her bed. We stayed in the kitchen to clean up and get ourselves ready for bed. All four of us slept in this small kitchen. There were two single beds for the four of us.

All through the evening we watched Father pacing the bedroom, hands in his pockets, his head nodding as though he was talking to himself. He didn't so much as look at us. Mother was lying in bed, and every few minutes he would go over to her, hold her hand for a moment, and then begin to pace the room again. Just before we crawled into bed, he walked in and told us that he had to go out, but we shouldn't worry because he would be right back. When he returned, he had a woman with him. He explained that this woman would help Mother have the baby. My sisters and I tried to fall asleep, but we couldn't.

Mother was going to have a baby! I was the oldest, and even though it had been explained to me how babies were born, I couldn't comprehend. I definitely couldn't tell my younger sisters what was happening. Father came into the kitchen and sat on my bed. With tears in his eyes, he explained that God would give us a baby, hopefully a boy. He told us that he remembered the time when each of us was born, and that then, as now, he couldn't wait to see if it was a girl or a boy, and if Mother would come out of this difficult delivery healthy and happy. "I love you all," he tried to reassure us, and then he kissed us all good night. His eyes were filled with tears as he walked out of the kitchen. "Please go to sleep, my darlings," he whispered. "It might take time for the baby to come."

Morning came, and we were awakened by a scream: "It's a boy! It's a boy!" When I peeked into the bedroom, I saw my father looking taller than ever. He wore the biggest smile I'd ever seen on his face, and his eyes were shining. We rushed into the bedroom. Mother was lying on the bed, looking so peaceful and fragile. We came near the bed, and she pointed to the tiny creature resting in her arms. We looked and looked at this little baby, unable to understand how it had come into being and where it had come from. We smiled at our dear mother and rushed back into the kitchen.

All four of us held hands and began to sing: "It's a boy! It's a boy! We have a brother!" Father came in with the baby in his arms, stepped into the circle and joined us in our singing.

It was almost midnight when I shook myself out of the past. It was memories such as these that tortured all of us. Every night one or more of my sisters would wake up screaming, crying, looking for Mother, Father, and Moshe. Many nights we would all wake up and try to console each other.

The long first night in our new house in Prachatice finally ended, and morning dawned. I rushed to see how Anna was feeling, and fortunately she was much better. She was ready to jump out of bed and look through this new house. I begged my other sisters to take care of her and not let her do too much, for I had to run off to work.

The office was very close to our new home, and I was

there at nine o'clock sharp. The officer greeted me kindly
and assigned me a large desk with a typewriter on it. I had
learned how to type in high school, but I hadn't seen or used
a typewriter in many years. Nevertheless, I had high hopes.
My job was to interpret between the Americans and the
Czechs for as long as the Americans occupied Czechoslovakia. I went to work day after day, and I was so glad I had
this job.

My desk was always cluttered with papers, and my office
full of people. The Czechs were having a difficult time
adjusting to freedom and were grateful for any help that was
offered. They had been occupied for such a long time, first
by the Germans, and now by the Americans. There were so
many displaced people. Factories and businesses were at a
standstill, and many men hadn't returned from the war yet. I
loved working for the Czech people. The sun was beginning
to shine for them, and they were slowly recovering from war,
beginning to enjoy freedom.

My sisters and I were having an equally difficult time
adjusting to freedom. We tried to understand that we were
free at last, but the years of imprisonment were not easy to
leave behind. Every day, after I came home from work, I
taught my sisters English. I brought books for them to read.
They studied very hard. We now had enough food, for I
could get anything I wanted from the PX, the American
Army's food warehouse. Some days I would bring enough
food to last for a week, but it would all be gone the next day!
Our passion for food was tremendous. We marveled at the
strange American delights: peanut butter, ham and raisins,
popcorn. We often overate and got painful stomachaches and
diarrhea. Slowly, we learned to deal with this problem also.
Sometimes our Czech neighbors would bring us fresh fruit
and vegetables. They were polite and offered help, but . . .
they were total strangers. They could in no way understand
what we had lived through.

One night, we were sitting around the table finishing
dinner, and we had a big argument about what to do, about
how to deal with our freedom. "What else *can* we do?" Anna

asked. "We have a roof over our heads, we have enough food, we have a lovely garden; why can't we just stay here?"

"How can we stay here?" Pola shouted. "The Germans will come and get us."

Mania agreed. "Pola is right. Let's go back to Poland, let's return to Jelesnia. Maybe we'll find Mother and Father there. Who knows if they really died? Maybe they are still alive."

"You are such a dreamer," Pola shot back angrily. "And how do you think we could get to Poland? Should we walk there? Even if we could do it, they wouldn't let us in. Don't you know yet, Poland has declared all the Jewish people stateless? We are not Polish anymore. Poland doesn't want us."

I listened to all the talk. I couldn't imagine what we could do, or to whom we could turn. During the day, as at bedtime, the nightmares never stopped. The screams tore at our hearts and bodies. All through the night I felt as if I was still in the camps, the electric fence around me, the guards with their machine guns pointed at me, and there was no escape. I tried to run, to free myself, but even in my dreams I couldn't find a way.

I survived, and yet . . . : My thoughts go back to the days of gloom, hunger, and cold. My body shivers, my stomach cramps, and yet . . . every vein tells me to go on. Where is it that I am alive? How is it that I keep on breathing? I keep on moving, working, talking, living, praying, hoping. It is the night that brings death, engulfs the dear ones, one by one. The darkness sets over Mother and Father, my little brother and so many friends, dead. A cold wind encircles me, chills my body. Millions have perished. I'm alone. And yet . . . an invisible power relieves me of my feelings, the texture of memory changes. A new desire to live, to breathe, to hope sets in. Another sunrise, another morning . . .

4. Maminka

My work kept me busy, and my days were filled with new people, all of whom were in need of help. There were so many displaced persons from this horrible war. One day the Czech mayor walked into my office. *"Sleczna,"* he called me. I remember it meant "nice lady." "I found a young girl—I'm almost sure she is Jewish, like you—but she doesn't know that the war is over. She escaped from the death march. She found a German farmer who seemed willing to help. He put her to work, but never told her that the war was over. Do you think you could give her a place to live?"

The next day, a hot July afternoon, he brought Lola to our house. We were all talking and trying to get to know each other when she mentioned that she loved to cook. My sisters and I were overjoyed, for not one of us liked to be in charge of the kitchen. And so we all agreed that Lola would live with us, and see to it that we would all be fed.

Lola was a good cook, but she was always afraid there wouldn't be enough food for tomorrow. She too had been starved in the concentration camps; she knew what it meant to be hungry. She would set a nice table with the pretty china we had found in the house, and we would all sit down to eat, reaching for the knives and forks. Then the aroma of the chicken would reach our noses, and we would grab it with our fingers and stuff it into our mouths. It was a perfect circus, each of us trying to speak with our mouths full, and usually Anna would burst out laughing. It must have been such a funny sight.

Lola was also a wonderful baker. She learned very quickly

that she couldn't bake while we were in the house, for if we could smell the cake, we would find it and devour it. She would never put all the food on the table; she had to put some away for a rainy day.

There was so much about Lola that we couldn't understand. She was always frightened. She would wake up in the middle of the night screaming and crying. We tried to console her—we wanted to help her as we had always helped each other—but she wouldn't confide in us. She simply couldn't talk about her past. The only thing we knew for sure was that she had gone through starvation, because she paid more attention to food than to anything else. We hoped that sooner or later she would share her pain with us.

One day I told Lola that I had invited ten American officers for a Sunday dinner. She almost fainted at the news. Every night that week she would give us less to eat, and she would put away some chicken for the big dinner. Unfortunately, we had no refrigeration. Sunday afternoon as we started to prepare the dinner, we noticed that some of the chicken was not so fresh. We put it up to our noses, sniffing the sour odor and trying to determine how bad it was. We decided that we would serve ourselves the smelly chicken, and give the fresh stuff to the Americans.

As we sat down to dinner that night, we started serving our guests first. But they were trying to be gentlemen and insisted that the ladies should be served first, and so they pushed the plates in front of us. I remember bursting into laughter, as we were pushing the plates back and forth. Our plan was foiled. I think it got to a point where we weren't sure who had what chicken, but we ate it all up.

We knew how much the Americans liked French fried potatoes, but Lola could not bring herself to use the whole can of lard we had received for our weekly rations. Deep frying was out of the question as far as she was concerned. "So what if they eat plain fried potatoes?" She was adamant, and fried potatoes were served.

After we had eaten, one of the officers offered a prayer in

gratitude for our survival. When he was finished, I offered a prayer of my own:

"Thank you with all my heart for coming to Europe to fight this war. I know it cannot be easy for a young man to leave his family and come so far to fight. But the war was long, much too long, and millions of innocent people had already died. We are the lucky ones who survived, and it was only because you came and liberated us, not a moment too soon. Death and starvation constantly surrounded us. Our parents, our brother, and so many of our relatives and friends were killed; there was very little hope for us to survive."

I couldn't stop; the words were flowing like they never had before: "We understand that we are free now, but you have to keep reassuring us that we are indeed free. We are still in a strange land, far away from home, with hardly any hope of being able to return to Poland. We know that we are definitely not wanted there; we've already heard that Poland doesn't want Jewish people to return to their homes. We would all love to go to America, for it is you Americans who have given us life and a new beginning." I finished with tears in my eyes.

There was silence in the room. I got up from my chair and went around kissing each of our guests. To this day, all these years later, their faces are engraved in my mind, although some of their names are lost. A few of these men remained our friends for years; others, while never seen again, remained in our hearts.

Each day brought something new into our lives. My English was getting better, and I could express myself well. My sister Pola had already learned enough English to be able to work in the supply office. She told me that having a job made her feel wanted and needed, appreciated as a human being again, and not just a number. In fact, she began to cover her tattoo with a bandage every day so as not to be reminded of those awful days. Mania kept busy mending and fixing clothes for us. Anna was growing up; she didn't look like that skinny fifteen-year-old girl anymore. She was looking bigger and healthier each day. She helped Lola keep house and she kept track of what everybody did and how they did it. We all had to learn again how to eat, how to talk to people, and most especially how to laugh.

The six years of persecution had taken away from us the basic rules of living. We had to learn to live without our parents. We were orphans who would never again feel the loving touch of a mother or father. We would never see them again. Still, we considered ourselves blessed, for we four sisters were together; we had each other. Gienia was more and more like our sister each day, and when Lola joined us, she too became a part of our family.

Lola had been living with us for a couple of months when she asked me to take her to the farm where she had been tricked into believing that the war was still going on. I had a car at my disposal and the driver took us there. During the ride, Lola began to tell me what life had been like for her on the farm. She whispered to me, not wanting the driver to hear a word she said. She escaped from the death march, she told me, and hid in a barn, very much like my sisters and I had done. The farmer found her asleep in the barn, and she pretended to be a Polish girl, lost and looking for work. She told me that the farmer had worked her very hard, fed her little, and abused her regularly. She worked there for four months before the mayor came and took her away. Tears were rolling down Lola's face for the first time since I had known her.

When we arrived at the farm, I walked with her to the front door. A young woman opened the door, but Lola wouldn't say a word. She just stood there looking at the woman. I think she was still afraid that the farmer might come and hurt her. The idea of being free, of the war being over, hadn't penetrated her being yet. Suddenly the farmer appeared behind his wife, and Lola turned and ran back to the car without a word. I stayed my ground and confronted the farmer: How he could have kept Lola, and made her work so hard for nothing, when he knew the war was over? The two of them only looked at me, and didn't say a word. I joined Lola in the car and motioned the driver to return home. Neither Lola nor I were able to express any hatred toward these people. We didn't allow ourselves to feel more hate. The war was over.

One Sunday morning, Anna and I were out for a walk, and we spotted a young girl, all alone. As we came closer, we recognized her; she had been with us in one of the concentration camps. We were stunned by her appearance. Her face was painted with lipstick and rouge, and she had on a strange dress that hardly covered her body.

"Stella, what happened to you? You look like a whore!" Anna was practically yelling at her. Stella just hung her head. She wouldn't look either one of us in the eyes. She must be one of the girls that the Czech mayor had told me about, I realized. He had said that some of our women were serving the sexual needs of the Americans for whatever they could get in return. Anna and I exchanged glances and we knew that we had to do something for Stella.

"You must come and live with us," Anna insisted. I was taken aback; I felt that I already had enough responsibilities. But I couldn't say no to this girl who so obviously needed help, and so we took Stella into our home. The only room left was close to the exit door. I told Stella that if she ever tried to bring any soldiers into her bedroom, she could pack her few belongings and close the door behind her forever.

Each of the members of the household assumed a role in the family; Anna was the self-appointed watchdog of our brood. She was very suspicious of Stella, and was convinced that before long she would break the rule. She decided to spy on her. One night she placed a heavy iron on Stella's window sill. In the middle of the night, we were all awakened by a loud crashing noise. We came running just in time to see a man leaving Stella's room.

I rushed into the room, followed by my sisters, and found Stella cowering on the bed. I was furious. "Stella," I scolded, "you know that we have rules in this house. This is not the kind of behavior I want happening here. If I ever find another soldier in this house at night, you will have to leave."

The next morning, we discussed our growing family. It was clear that we needed someone to head the family and impose order. From that moment on, my family of sisters began calling me *Maminka*, which meant "Mother" in Czech. While this added to their security, it tremendously increased my feeling of responsibility. It looked like we were a very happy family at times, but beneath the surface our psychological needs were overwhelming.

For me, prayer was an important part of life. I tried to teach the girls different prayers in Polish and in Hebrew, and asked them to join me in prayer every night. They found it very difficult. Pola would question: "Why are we praying to God? What did God do for our mother and father, and our little brother?"

"Where was God when six million Jewish people were slaughtered?" Anna would protest.

Gienia would chime in: "How can we build faith in God? Didn't He abandon us?"

I couldn't find an answer to these difficult questions, and yet my faith in God grew stronger with each day. I would look around me and see my sisters and the other young people who lived with us, and all I could think of was that we were alive, we had survived, and we could all look forward to a wonderful future.

I went to work every morning and interviewed other survivors; each day I faced the difficult task of finding places for them to live. But I always tried to instill in them some faith in the future. For me there was God and always will be. My own faith was never shaken, even though I couldn't find the answers to my sisters' questions.

Each of us struggled, but we could always rely on the others in times of need. We were a family. We formed great friendships. Our basic needs were met, and yet as the weeks and months went by, we became aware of a terrible feeling of loneliness. We realized that all of this living and laughing was very superficial. We were all just trying to kill time; we tried not to think of our present, or our future. Our past was too painful. Here we were, in a small town in Czechoslovakia, an island of adolescents in the middle of a foreign country, among complete strangers; we simply didn't belong here. We had a house, but it wasn't a home, and it wasn't even ours. It was just a temporary loan given to us by the Czech mayor.

"How long will they let us stay here?" Pola said on our way to work one day. "What will happen? What if the American occupation forces leave Czechoslovakia? I've heard rumors that they're going to leave soon," she added, growing more and more agitated. "How long after the Americans leave before the Czechs evict us and send us away?" She was practically screaming now.

I listened to her questions and I was touched by the fear she was expressing, yet I couldn't find the words to ease her pain. I had no answers. That night, I lay awake in my bed and I kept hearing Pola's questions over and over in my head. I was having nightmares even though I wasn't sleeping. Finally I turned to God, and with a prayer on my lips, I closed my eyes, waiting for another sunrise, another morning.

5. *Kurt: A Boy's Story*

We were not the only young people who had survived the war. Almost every day the Czech official came into my office with another problem. So many young girls and boys were still hiding from the Germans.

I was at my desk one morning when the secretary from the mayor's office walked in. *"Sleczna,"* she told me, "we have a little boy. He is like you, *Yevrei* (Jewish). He says that he is thirteen or fourteen years old and he is all alone. Could you do something for him?"

She turned and motioned for the boy to join us. He was a short fellow, young but wizened.

"What is your name?" I asked.

He said nothing.

"You do have a name, don't you?" I repeated.

He remained motionless, his eyes filled with fear.

Finally, he whispered: "Kurt."

"Well, Kurt, we'll have to find a home for you. Why don't you wait here for me. I'll try to finish work early and perhaps I can take you to my home. How about it?"

I thought to myself, "My sisters will kill me."

The Czech secretary thanked me and left Kurt in my care. The young man didn't say much on our way home, but when I started asking questions, I realized how his background differed from ours. He was a German Jew, from Berlin. On our way to the house, his fear was evident. When he saw a man walking down the street he said: "Is he a Nazi? Can he arrest me?" For Kurt the war was still on. He was

38

constantly watching, turning his head to listen, always ready for the unexpected.

I explained to Kurt that I had three natural sisters, but that there were three other girls living with us, who were a part of our family. "You will be the only man in the family," I told him.

When we got to the house I called out: "Children! Children! I have a surprise for you!"

Everyone came running in and looked at this strange fellow. Anna pointed at Kurt. "This, this!" she blurted out, bursting into laughter. She couldn't believe that I would bring a boy to live with us. The others were surprised, too, and I had a hard time getting them settled down so that Kurt would have a chance to tell his story. We soon discovered, however, that he had no intention of telling us anything.

"Why should I trust you?" he asked. There was so much about Kurt that was typical of most of the survivors. He was alone. He was fearful of everyone and everything. Before he spoke, he looked behind the drapes and the doors. When he ate, he turned the food over and over on his plate, uncertain that it was real food.

"You're safe with us," I tried to assure him. "The Americans are everywhere. The Germans can't hurt you anymore."

After a time, Kurt began to trust us, chiefly because he had no one else to turn to. One day he began to tell us what he remembered. His father and mother had been arrested at their home in Berlin the day after *Kristallnacht* in November 1938. Kristallnacht, the "night of glass," was the night when the hatred of the Jews that had been building in Germany erupted into mass violence. Nazi sympathizers ran through the cities, smashing all the Jewish storekeepers' windows, looting and burning stores and synagogues.

After his parents' arrest, Kurt and his sister were left home alone; they waited and waited and waited for their parents to come back. Kurt was eight years old and his sister ten. The neighbors looked after them until one day the Nazis rounded up all the Jewish children and transported them on trucks somewhere away from home. Kurt was separated from his sister and many days later arrived in Auschwitz. Most of the children on the transport trucks didn't speak his language. When they arrived in Auschwitz one of the SS men asked him a question, and when he answered in German the man pulled him aside. From that day until the Russians liberated the camp in January 1945, Kurt lived with the SS man.

Kurt stopped talking and just stared into space. I came to his side and put my arm around him. "What is it you are thinking about?" I asked him gently.

"Well, I don't know if I can tell you," he whispered. "Maybe I can explain it just to you, Ruth; could I?"

"Come on, all of you, get out of here. Kurt and I have to talk," I said, motioning the girls out of the room.

Kurt and I sat on his bed and he proceeded: "What was I supposed to do? If I hadn't stayed with him I would have been put in the oven with all the others." He paused. "You don't understand, do you?"

I was puzzled.

"He told me I was a pretty boy, and he used me," Kurt went on, hesitantly. "I had to do everything he wanted me to do. *Everything*, I had no choice. When he wanted a favor from someone, he would send me. I had to please them so he could get what he wanted. He was good to me sometimes, and other times he beat me really hard. I saw him kill two boys. I couldn't save them. You won't tell anyone, will you? I hope you'll never tell."

How well I understood now. "Oh Kurt, how I wish I could help you to forget all that has happened to you. You're so young, and you've had to live through so much. Your mother and father didn't leave you because they didn't love you. The Nazis took them away because they were Jewish; there was nothing you could have done to stop it. How awful it must have been for you. The time you spent in this most horrible camp, Auschwitz, you had no choice but to do what you had to do. Perhaps God wanted to save you. So few Jewish children survived, and look at you: a wonderful fourteen-year-old boy. You have a whole future ahead of you. Hopefully, we can find your parents and you'll be reunited with them. You never know. . . . You are so young, please try to forget this terrible past and begin a new life. I know you will."

Kurt began to cry and I put his head on my chest and felt like crying with him. We were both so young and yet so old. What Kurt had lived through would remain with me forever.

A few days after we had our talk, Kurt asked me to write a letter to his uncle. "Maminka, please write a letter to my uncle Speiser in Buenos Aires, please, please," he begged.

How could I address a letter to Uncle Speiser, Buenos Aires, Argentina? One day I shared my worry with the chaplain on the base, and he advised me to send the letter APO (army post office) to the Jewish Community in Buenos Aires. I did just that. I wrote all about Kurt, included our APO address, and, with a prayer for Kurt, I sent my letter off in search of Uncle Speiser.

Part Two
Relief and Rehabilitation

6. *UNRRA and the DP Camps*

By the end of August, 1945, the American occupation forces were preparing to move out of Czechoslovakia. The officer in charge asked me to detail my plans for the future. I broke into tears trying to explain to him that there was no future for me, nor for my sisters. This was not my country; this was not my home.

"I think that as soon as the Americans leave, the Czechs will take the house we live in away from us, and we'll be in the street again. We have no place to go and no one to turn to," I told the officer.

"I could get a job for you in Germany," he suggested. "Our army will stay there for a while."

"In Germany? How can we go back to Germany? The Nazis will kill us for sure."

"The war is over. Don't you know it yet? Nothing can happen to you now. You are free! Besides, the job that I had in mind is with the United Nations."

He sounded so reassuring that I finally nodded my head. The next morning he wrote a letter of recommendation to the Civil Affairs Detachment and UNRRA (United Nations Relief and Rehabilitation Administration) in Tirschenreuth, Germany. I have kept this letter all these years, for it was the genesis of yet another new phase of my life.

* * *

Headquarters 94th Infantry Division
Civil Affairs Section
8 August, 1945

Subject: Recommendation

To: Whom it may concern

Miss Ruth Ferber has worked with the Civil Affairs Det. under the operational jurisdiction of Civil Affairs Section 94th Infantry Division from June 18, 1945, to the present date. Her services have been most satisfactory, and her performance of duty excellent. She has been very attentive towards her work and has proven to be a definite asset to Civil Affairs relations between the American forces and the Czech people.

Her knowledge of the English, German, Russian, Polish, Czech, and Hebrew languages has been an invaluable aid. Miss Ruth Ferber is recommended without hesitancy to the Civil Affairs Detachment and UNRRA Team in Tirschenreuth.

Reuben F. Hammer
1st Lt. FA
Asst. Div. C.A.O.

Within a week I was notified that I'd have a position with the UNRRA Team 168, in Tirschenreuth, Germany.

Getting ready to leave wasn't difficult because we had so few belongings, but saying goodbye to the ghosts in our house was very hard. We were, however, ready to leave when the truck arrived.

We climbed aboard in complete silence. Suddenly Anna started screaming: "I'm not going! Trucks take people to the gas chambers! I'm not going!" She jumped off the truck. Kurt, too, balked at this voyage; he knew trucks took children to Auschwitz to die. My own heart was heavy, too, at the prospect of going back to Germany, but since I had been working with the Americans I was beginning to realize that we could trust them, and that the war was truly over. We didn't have to fear the Germans anymore. Somehow I had to convince Kurt and my sisters.

I begged them to get onto the truck and asked them to imagine this beautiful place we were moving to: Tirschenreuth, a city in the mountains, a place like our home, so many years ago. I spoke of the beautiful home we were going to have there, maybe even with a pool. I tried to instill some positive thinking in them, in spite of the fact that I myself had no idea where Tirschenreuth was or what it would look like.

I was finally able to convince them to get on the truck, and the driver handed us some candy. Our spirits lightened, and as the truck began to roll, we all started to sing. We sang some Polish songs. It all seemed to work for a while, and yet for the rest of the trip I was wondering: Will the fear ever stop? Will we ever fall asleep at night and not worry about waking up in the morning? Will we ever be able to laugh? Will our time to live, to love, to enjoy life ever come?

"Why don't we go home?" Mania kept asking. "What are we waiting for? Maybe Father survived and he is looking for us in Jelesnia?"

"Let's be patient, my darling," I would tell her. "Perhaps one day we'll be able to return home, but for now we'll have a place to live and we will all be together."

We arrived at Tirschenreuth in the evening. A house was provided for us by UNRRA. Knowing that this organization was formed by the United Nations to give help to the thousands of displaced persons all over Europe gave us a sense of security. We went to sleep, thanking God for letting us reach this place.

I got up early in the morning and my sisters were still sleeping when I was leaving for work. Little Kurt was up, and he wished me good luck with my new job. I certainly needed it; there was so much to learn. I arrived in the office and was introduced to all sorts of people. There was a young lady from Denmark, another from Sweden, and Dorothy Jones from America, with whom I was to work.

The office was located in the middle of a large camp. It was a former concentration camp. The war was over, and yet thousands of people were still housed in the same horrible barracks they had lived in throughout the war. Even though the wire barricades were gone and the SS guards were no longer there, the people couldn't move about freely. Deprived of their basic needs, they found it difficult to deal with normal physical and psychological functions. Many of them had lost the sense of responsibility and even the desire to build a new life. Having survived Hitler's hell, they were now waiting for a miracle. They expected the world to open its arms and doors and take them in, to offer relief, to pay them for all their sufferings, to give them freedom, a home, a place to live and breathe freely.

An urgent need for rehabilitation was evident throughout Germany. The United Nations organization had realized this, and the United Nations Relief and Rehabilitation Administration was organized in 1945 to assist other groups and organizations helping the displaced persons, such as the Red Cross, American Joint Distribution Committee, Catholic Welfare, American Friends Service Committee, and others. At first UNRRA personnel worked with the American Army in the DP (displaced persons) camps; the eventual goal was for them to replace the army personnel and administer the camps alone.

The UNRRA team consisted mainly of social workers and administrative personnel from forty-six countries all over the world. In addition to their social work qualifications, the volunteers were required to speak both English and German. Despite these requirements, the hurriedly-picked UNRRA volunteers were not really prepared for the enormous task that awaited them. They didn't have any understanding of what the survivors had been through, and often didn't speak their language. There was not only a tremendous language barrier, but also a lack of understanding of various cultural backgrounds.

The needs of the survivors were frequently misunderstood by the UNRRA personnel. The kinds of problems they had to deal with were staggering, and neither books nor history had taught anyone how to cope with these people who had been victimized and deprived of all their human rights.

Many of the survivors had their names stolen and instead had numbers printed on their arms. Their hair was shaven and they hardly had enough clothing to cover their bony bodies. The hunger and starvation they had suffered through the years awakened in them such a craving for food that nothing could stop them from stealing and grabbing it whenever the opportunity arose. These were people who really had been robbed of their character and personhood.

The UNRRA personnel ran into these psychological stone walls, and sought to employ people from the community of survivors, who were well acquainted with the past and certainly with the current problems that these multitudes faced. I was one of the first survivors to be employed. When I finally met the director, Stanley B. Milus, he was surprised that I wanted to work with the displaced persons, considering the horrors I had lived through.

"Are you sure you can work with these people, who for the most part have lived through the same experiences you did? Will you be able to sleep at night, knowing and understanding the difficulties they are facing now? Do you want to re-live the camps?" He was obviously concerned, and I was touched.

"I know that it won't be easy," I answered, "but if I can help in any way possible, I know that God saved me to do just that."

I started to work immediately. I began as a secretary to Mr. Milus, but soon took over many administrative duties. It was a difficult task indeed, dealing with thousands of people who had lived through so many tragedies, and such unbelievable atrocities, who had miraculously survived, only to continue to live in barracks with stringent limitations. At first men and women had to live in separate barracks. It was a long time before husbands and wives could even find quarters where they could at least sleep together at night.

For many of the Jewish survivors, help was too little, too late. Many Jews who had managed to survive the war were still lying naked on the bunk beds of concentration camps; they were breathing, but not much more. One day, I walked into such a camp in Furth, Germany, and a young girl, her head bald, her body emaciated, looked up at me from her bed and tried to lift herself to hug me. "Help me! Help me!" she cried out in agony. She fell back, unable to move. I had her transferred to a hospital and fortunately she recovered.

Others were not so lucky. Many died of starvation even though they had managed to stay alive until the end of the war. There was the fourteen-year-old girl who devoured grass, for her hunger was so painful, and died of dehydration from the diarrhea that emptied her insides. She had starved for years in concentration camps, and now lost her battle just a few weeks after the war was over.

One of the most painful missions that I had to conduct was funerals for those who died after the war was over. My friend the American chaplain, Rabbi Eugene Lipman, conducted services for the dead, and I stood by him and interpreted for those who attended. "Magnified and sancti-fied be Thy name, oh God," he chanted in English and sometimes in Hebrew. "Blessed be Thou, oh Lord, our God," he kept repeating. But the young childen in the caskets could not raise their voices to the skies and bless God, who had seemingly forsaken them.

No, the dead cannot bless God; neither can those whose suffering is beyond their comprehension. So many had seen their loved ones killed before their eyes, had their little children shot right in their arms. Many had their mates taken away from them in the prime of life. No, they couldn't bless God. Then there were those who had retained their faith in God through all their suffering. They believed their faith had helped them to escape death.

But escaping death was only the beginning for these people. Now they had to learn to live again. There was spring in the air. They could breathe, they could see, and they could touch. They wanted to fight their way back to life, to find shelter, food, and clothing, but there was no way for them to regain any independence. They had to remain in the DP camps. They had to live and sleep in barracks.

The outside world was not friendly to them. The Germans closed their doors to the displaced persons and certainly to the Jewish survivors. They were afraid to look at the rags of humanity they had created. Some were afraid they would come face to face with those they had tortured and almost killed. Indeed, they had many reasons to be afraid, but although they had lost the war, they were not the losers. They were free: free to move, to live, to carry on with their lives. They had returned to their homes and their families. For the Jewish survivors and many others, there was no home to return to and no family to come back to. It would be a long time before some of the European countries and the United States opened their doors to take in some of the survivors.

In the meantime, something had to be done for all these people in the camps. The camp I had been assigned to consisted mainly of adults; there were very few children among them, and most of these were non-Jews, as nearly all the Jewish children in the concentration camps had been murdered during the war. After a short time I organized a school for these DP children. They were always my greatest concern. Ever since I had heard that over a million children had been killed, I knew that I had to do everything I could for children wherever they lived.

The parents insisted that the children be taught in their own language, which meant six different languages: Polish, Czech, Hungarian, Ukrainian, Latvian, and Lithuanian. Teachers of these nationalities were hard to find. Books were also in short supply; the camp residents had to translate the few German books we had into their own languages. I even wrote to the public schools in New York to get textbooks, which the DPs also had to translate. This was a long and arduous process; the people at the camp translated the books on any paper we could find, and the makeshift books were then passed from one class to the next. The struggle for materials as simple as paper and pencils went on forever.

Every time I walked into a classroom, I heard the cries for school supplies. I also heard cries for food. The rations were still inadequate and many times the children would go to bed hungry.

I invited local ministers and priests to teach the young people religion. (No, I didn't forget the rabbis, but there were hardly any Jewish children left in the camps after the war. They had disappeared in the gas chambers of Auschwitz.) They had a hard time building hope and faith in these children who were still living in camps, sharing their beds with their parents, never knowing what the next day would bring.

One of the important things for the children to learn was the sense of belonging to a family, to the community, to the country from which they were displaced. Getting rid of the fear and getting them to recognize that they were free proved to be extremely difficult. Many children had speech impediments. These children had been forced into silence out of fear. Their parents had oftentimes forbidden them to speak, for fear they might say something for which the Germans would kill them.

The problems were staggering, and our team was expanded to try to meet the many needs. We now had social workers, child care officers, counselors, and delegates from many nations who were trained professionals. Yet how little these trained professionals knew about the needs of the survivors! They were willing to help, but they didn't have the experience. I did. I had lived through hell and come out of it. I had died a thousand times and survived, just as the other displaced persons had. I knew what made them tick; I felt what they felt.

Each day for us was a new discovery. All things were new: food, clothes, relationships, simply living and breathing. There were the joys of washing and combing out our hair, which was just beginning to grow back. Even everyday chores were a pleasure, although strange to us. What an adventure it was to eat a meal, to sit at a table, to reach for a fork or a knife, to swallow a divine piece of chicken or boiled potato, to say nothing of a piece of cake or a sliver of precious chocolate. We used to say *"niebo w gebie* (heaven in the mouth).'' Those who have not experienced starvation cannot imagine what it's like to go without food for days, to live from one day to the next on a few sips of thin soup or a meager slice of bread, knowing that one small bite of food may determine whether you live to see the next sunrise. The mere memory of those days makes me shiver. It makes me feel hungry. Even now, after so many years, the memory of those days moves my tongue in need of food. I don't think I'll ever be able to forget this feeling.

Meals carried another wonderful meaning as well: relating to people. There was a great need to relate to others, to share, to listen, and to talk. In the camps you could hardly share anything with anybody, not even your own sisters. Suddenly the options were there. There was no more worry about being reported. You could say anything, sometimes just for the sake of hearing yourself speak. Get it out of your system, get it off your chest, we all urged each other. There was so much hurt hidden inside, so much pain. It was hard to get it out. Everyone was filled with sorrow; everyone had lost someone dear, someone close.

When families were torn apart during the war, there was no time to mourn, but now the survivor had the time to reflect and to miss mother, father, sister, or brother. My youngest sister, Anna, missed Mother terribly and every night she woke us up with screams and nightmares that never seemed to end. We all mourned our little brother, who had been the joy of the family. We had all sorts of affectionate nicknames for him: we called him Monius, Monyush, Mojs-hele. "My youngest child is a boy!" Father used to brag. And this youngest child, the only son, was gassed in Auschwitz at the tender age of eleven.

My sisters and I talked about Moshe, but we found it very difficult to talk about Mother and Father. We knew that Mother's life had ended in the same gas chambers as our brother's, but we were not really sure what had happened to Father. Then one day, I was sitting in my office, and a young

53

man from Krakow came to me with some problems. When I told him I had lived in Krakow, he said that he was in Mauthausen concentration camp with some other men from Krakow. One of the men he mentioned was Aaron Ferber, my father. A chill ran up and down my spine. I was scared to ask. The young man was surprised to learn that he had known my father. He hesitated, but eventually told me what he knew: my father, at the age of forty-two, had died of starvation at Mauthausen just three days before the end of the war.

The most difficult part of it was that I had to bring the news to my sisters. There was no doubt now: Father was dead. We really were orphans.

7. The Pain of Memory

That night I wished I didn't have to go home. I couldn't possibly imagine how I was going to tell my sisters that Father was dead. I pictured Mania, who kept saying we should go back home, for Father would certainly be there waiting for us. And Anna, who never stopped telling stories about Father. She was the youngest of us four girls, and before our little brother was born, Father treated her like a boy. He took her horseback riding, he climbed mountains with her—she was definitely Daddy's little girl. Pola had doubts about Father being alive, as I had had. After all, he was shipped out of Plaszow with thousands of other inmates, and as far as we knew, hardly anyone had survived. Still, we all dreamed about him being alive. And now, this horrible truth. What was I to do?

Dinner was ready when I arrived at our house, and we all sat around the table quietly. This was very unusual, for most of the time the girls couldn't wait to tell me what they had done that day. Kurt started saying something, but trailed off, complaining, "Nobody wants to listen to me." That was the extent of our dinner conversation that night. We were all involved in our own thoughts.

Finally, Lola broke the silence. "Well, how did you like my meatballs?" she asked. "What is the matter with you, Ruth? Why don't you eat?"

I leapt up from my chair, unable to hold back my tears. I ran to my bedroom and buried my face in my pillow.

My sisters followed me, clamoring for an explanation.

55

"What happened? Why don't you tell us? Please, please, tell us what's wrong!"

I pulled myself together, and, raising myself to a sitting position, I motioned for my sisters to join me on the bed. "I must tell you something, but it's very sad. I don't know how to tell you this. Promise me you won't go crazy. We have been through so much already. But we are alive! We are together! And we love each other." My sisters fell silent, suddenly solemn. "We know that our dear mother died in Auschwitz, and so did Mojshele," I went on. "Until now we've been hoping that we would find Father. But that is the problem, that is why I am so sad tonight. I have learned that our father died of starvation three days before the end of the war, in Mauthausen. There was a man in my office today who knew Father, and he told me the terrible news."

Mania started crying violently, and both Pola and Anna were shaking their heads. "I don't believe it, I can't believe it!" they shouted. "He was so young and so strong; he was only forty-two! How could he die of hunger? He always managed, all through the years in Plaszow, even though he had to share his rations with Mojshele. Somehow he went on living and working. No, no, it can't be true!"

For a moment my sisters' disbelief took hold of me, too: maybe the man in my office had been wrong! Father was young and strong . . . But the man had seen Father, he saw his body; he knew he was dead. The only thing left for us was to accept the horrible truth, and to go on living, for that is what Father would have wanted us to do.

That night we all went to sleep with heavy hearts.

I was fast asleep when I was awakened by someone crawling into my bed. This wasn't such an unusual occurrence; my sisters often came into my room after a nightmare. I opened my eyes groggily; this time it was Mania.

"I have to talk to you," she whispered. "I'm sorry I woke you up. But now that Father is gone, too, I don't know what to think. I've never gotten over the fact that we could have saved Mother, and now we have no one."

"What are you talking about? How could we have saved Mother?" I couldn't imagine what she was talking about.

"I believe that we could have saved Mother from Auschwitz," she told me gravely. "Remember? When we arrived with thousands of other women from Plaszow? There was a segregation, right off the train, and some of the women were separated out and taken to the gas chambers. But we felt so very lucky, because the five of us—you, me, Pola, Anna, and Mother—managed to walk away from the train together. Mother was so happy. She told us we would never be separated again.

"Remember? We were all brought in front of a bathhouse and told to take off our clothes and leave our belongings on the lawn. There must have been five thousand women left, after the first segregation. Five thousand naked bodies, pulling, pushing, not knowing what to expect. We all thought that we were going to the gas chambers, remember? We held on to each other. We saw people pushing here and there, moving towards the bathhouse, but we had the feeling that as long as we were outside, we would stay alive and together. Finally, though," Mania frowned, "we had to move towards the bathhouse. When we came close to the entrance, two big SS guards were standing there. The women were talking in low, hushed voices. I couldn't believe what they were saying. 'He's here,' I heard someone whisper, 'Dr. Mengele is here.' I looked around and there he was. Are you listening to me?" Mania asked, tugging on my arm.

"I'm listening," I said dully, although my eyes had glazed over at the mention of the name. "I remember Dr. Mengele. He was the one who did all the segregations, who decided who would live and who would die. He was the one who performed all those horrible medical experiments. The ones who wound up in his laboratory could only wish they had already died."

"Well," Mania took a deep breath, "I believe that if we hadn't held back—if we had pushed our way to the bathhouse sooner, before Mengele got there—Mother would have stayed with us, she would have lived. But the moment we came close to the door, Mengele was already there, and he pushed Mother to the side. At the same moment, the other SS guard pushed the rest of us inside. I remember that Anna was holding your hand, and she tried to follow Mother, but the guard wouldn't let her. Only Mengele selected people for the gas.

"And so Mother was separated from us, and that night she burned with thousands of other women from Plaszow. I should have gone with her. I can never forgive myself. If only we had gotten to the bathhouse sooner. . . . I don't know what to think, but I can't forget this, and I can't forgive myself. I could have saved her, Ruth, and I miss her so much. I hope God will forgive me. And now this crazy story about Father. I can't believe it. He was so young, and so wonderful, and now we'll never see him again. Ruth, please help me, I can't go on like this," she pleaded, dissolving into tears.

I put my arms around her and kissed her tenderly. "Listen, my darling, you couldn't do anything to save Mother, that's for sure. There were segregations from the first moment we got to Auschwitz, and they were taking all the older women. It was inevitable that they were going to pick out Mother sooner or later. Nobody, but nobody, could have saved her. Try to forget about it, Mania. Mother loved you so much. She loved the clothes you made for her; she was always proud of you. She wouldn't want you to live with this horrible pain.

"It seems like our suffering will never end, doesn't it? And now, this story about Father. . . . But we are still together. God has granted us life. Let's look to the future. Maybe we can build a beautiful life for ourselves. I know that our parents would have been very proud of us. Go to sleep now, my dear, and don't wake the girls up." We kissed each other good night, and as she left my room I whispered, "I love you."

I knew that I would have to deal with Pola and Anna also, but in the meantime, I had to get some sleep. I was so drained, I couldn't wait to close my eyes again. But sleep wouldn't come. I could very well imagine how Father must have suffered. I knew what starvation did to a human being. I could see him struggling, trying to go on another day—another hour, even. But in the end, his efforts were in vain. My father, my dear, dear father, had died. How I wish I could have been with him before he closed his eyes forever. The sun's first rays were coming in my window when I finally found a little sleep.

The next morning I had to rush to the office, for there was so much for me to do and so many problems to be solved. I wondered at times if I would be able to deal with the enormity of it all.

8. Almost No Jewish Children Survived

The world always looks at children as something special. Children evoke protective emotions in people; they are the future. These principles didn't apply during the war, however. Why didn't the free countries of the world, including the United States of America, do anything to stop the terror, to stop the murder of one and a half million Jewish children?

After Kristallnacht, when it became apparent that Hitler's intentions towards the Jews were violent, some Americans did try to get permission for German refugee children to enter the United States. During the last week of May in 1939, the House of Representatives of the 76th Congress held a hearing before the Committee on Immigration and Naturalization. A Mr. Pickett of the American Friends Committee (Quakers) presented the following case:

"We present before you a grant of authority under specified conditions and nothing more. Under its terms authority is granted to admit to the US not more than 10,000 German children in excess of the present quota, during each of the calendar years 1939–1940. No child shall be eligible for admission who is over fourteen years of age, and no child may be admitted unless satisfactory assurances have been given by responsible private individuals, or by a responsible organization that the child will not be a public charge. This is the entire proposal—a grant of authority, permitting an emergency matter, the rescue from Germany of a limited number of children of tender years.

"The need for this measure is overwhelming. A catastrophe has occurred; unlike such a catastrophe as a fire or

60

earthquake, or tidal wave, which have commanded the help of America to unfortunates abroad so often in the past, the catastrophe threatens not only death, but a living death to thousands of children."

The Congressional response was a flat-out "No!" President Roosevelt was pressured by American public opinion to turn down this immigration request. Very few Jewish children survived the war. Those who managed to survive did so miraculously. A very few lived through the camps. Others found righteous Gentiles who would risk their own lives to hide a child all through the war. The young adults who survived and who had seen the atrocities, the killings, the murders, had great hopes and dreams of building a new and better world. To accomplish this goal they had to produce a new generation, and so having children was one of their immediate goals.

During the summer of 1946, we were faced with many pregnancies and then births in the DP camps. We had no facilities whatsoever, no room in the small hospital, no place for babies in the barracks. There were no clothes and not enough food for little babies.

The members of UNRRA were in confusion and great desperation. The question of abortion came up, but no solution was found. Some women went quietly to German doctors. In many cases the women themselves resorted to some old-fashioned ways of disposing of a fetus, and many women died of infection from their self-induced abortions.

I remember a couple of the UNRRA delegates came up with the idea of sterilization. I was, at the time, a child care officer, and the matter came into my hands. I'll never forget when I first received the proposal. Suddenly I felt as though I was in the concentration camp again. They were proposing to *sterilize* women who had gone through hell with their one hope being to survive, to live a normal life, to one day have babies, families! What a monstrous idea.

We called a large meeting; we had many arguments. I listened carefully to all they had to say, and it only confirmed my knowledge, my doubts about the ability of these UN-

RRA volunteers to deal with the insurmountable problems of the refugees. There was no doubt in my mind that they were *willing* to help. They gave of their time and money; they all meant well. But they hadn't seen the children burn. They hadn't seen the children shot in their mothers' arms. How could they understand this acute need to have children, to be fruitful and multiply? How could they? How could anyone who wasn't there?

The idea of sterilization was finally voted down in our area, and we went on having babies, delivering them as well as our own facilities allowed and trying to take care of them as best we could. Hundreds of children were born in the camps I worked in and in many displaced persons' camps all over Germany.

Soon, however, we discovered another problem. Women in concentration camps had been given something to stop them from menstruating. For some it was the herbs in the soup; for others it was simply starvation that made their bodies stop functioning normally. Now, the war was over, and still they didn't menstruate. Could they feel like women? Would they be able to have children? These questions were on the minds of many women, for all the survivors were of childbearing age. We were between the ages of fifteen and thirty-nine, perhaps as old as forty, but not older. Women over forty, like my own mother, had vanished. The Germans were constantly looking for "young, intelligent women" to do their impossibly hard labor. After the backbreaking work they had performed under starvation conditions, these young women now wondered whether their hormones would ever function again. Every month, in some cases for many years, the women waited for their periods to start; but for many it never happened, another medical and psychological problem to deal with.

There were wives who had lost their husbands, and husbands whose wives had been murdered. They were now stranded and all alone. How could they function sexually again? There were young girls who had kept their virginity for the moment of freedom, for the time when the war would

be over and they would be able to love. And then there were
some who even in the concentration camps had risked having
sex. In one of the camps a song was made up: *"Za zupke i za
kawalek chleba, dziewczeta dadza wszystko co trzeba i nie
trzeba"* ("For a cup of soup and a piece of bread the girls
will give anything"). And now, these girls were free; the war
was over. But they still lived in one long barrack with two
hundred other inhabitants. How could they experience sex?

I had a friend named Gita, who told me what it was like
for her. One day she was resting on her bunk bed among two
hundred other women, trying to comprehend what freedom
meant. How was it, she thought, that she didn't feel free?
Maybe because she was sharing her home with hundreds of
strangers; she couldn't have anything she wanted, and right
now she longed to have sex. In a sudden surge she jumped
off the bed and ran in the direction of the men's barracks.
The sun was throwing her shadow on the grass, and she
seemed bigger than she was. Her figure was slim, but she
extended her arms and stretched them to heaven, reaching
and grasping. Her feet carried her off the ground, and she
was almost suspended in the air. For one precious moment
she felt free. Her shadow couldn't hold her anymore, she
thought. She could move it. She could escape it in any
direction she wished. She could run straight into the men's
barracks and into Alex's arms. She could caress him, kiss
him, and perhaps make love to him. Today she felt the urge
to do it, to feel free at last.

With two hundred men around them, Alex held his
beloved in his arms. Certainly their movements were restricted, their lovemaking limited. They closed their eyes and
covered themselves with blankets. For a fleeting moment they
felt that they were the only two people there. There was a
greater meaning to the intercourse than just sex. Gita knew
that she shared her feelings with another person. She also
experienced an exhilarating emotional high and a release of
feelings she had kept tied in knots for so many years.

For some camp inhabitants, relationships grew into something more permanent. That, as far as I know, didn't happen

to Gita. Most of the young people her age believed that having intercourse was all right, but thinking about the consequences of open, unrestricted sex was the farthest thing from their minds. Many of the pregnancies we faced were completely unplanned, and we continued to struggle with the dilemma of caring for these new lives in such difficult conditions.

There were also other problems with children during this time. Hitler's aim had been to aid in the production of a pure Aryan race. A German woman who was willing to have a child with a blond, blue-eyed soldier was given all the free care she needed under the Nazi regime. At the same time, there were also German women who were infertile, and these women were given children who had been taken away from families within the borders of German-occupied countries. The program that was responsible for the distribution of these children to "good Aryan homes" was called the Children's Foster Home Program. There were thousands of children from all over Europe "given" to German families to be brought up as pure Germans.

My job as a child care officer took me into the lives of many such children who had been placed in these foster homes. Since the Germans were always orderly, meticulous records were kept, and when UNRRA recovered them it became our task to locate these missing children. Our aim was to reunite the children with their biological parents, if they were alive, or with their natural families. This was a painful and difficult job. I was so young, I didn't have maternal feelings yet, but I had seen so many children killed, so many children taken away from their mothers' arms and murdered. There were many nights when I lay awake trying to judge, trying to reason. What about this child? How will he or she feel? This child doesn't remember his parents. He was taken away when he was a baby, and now he is four or five years old. These are the only parents he knows. Where does he really belong? Should he be taken away from the only parents he knows? Then I would think: What about his real parents, his mother, the one who gave him life, and whose heart is broken forever? And how could we allow these innocent children to be brought up as Germans and perhaps one day have to kill their own people? My mind would jump back and forth, and I would spend the night sleepless and in the morning find myself no closer to an answer.

Once I was at work, I knew that emotions had to be kept for later. The order was: "Allied children must be reunited with their parents. The parent in Yugoslavia, Hungary, or Poland has the right to have the child back." Reasoning and logic had to help me when I entered a home and heard a child call "*Mutti*," meaning "Mother." Strength had to be on my side when the child held onto his mother's skirt and didn't want to leave, or when one seven-year-old boy, who was transported to a children's center for processing, left the center in the middle of the night and walked for days until he found the home from which he had been taken. That little boy was eventually reunited with his parents in Yugoslavia. Right or wrong, I may never know.

There were also the children in the displaced persons camps to think about. I had the good luck of working with two great American women, very devoted human beings. One was Dorothy Jones, and the other Catherine Hulme, author of *The Nun's Story* (a very well-known book of the time). Together we built schools and classrooms for the children. The Germans were in no way generous in giving us the facilities or the supplies. We requisitioned whatever material we could from the American army. We separated a part of the barracks with army parachutes, placed blankets on the floor, and seated the students close to each other. We had as many as six different nationalities in each classroom. Trying to reach them or teach them was no easy task. The children, however, were very eager to learn, and even more, they were delighted to be with other children. Their favorite subject was arts and crafts, and it wasn't long before they all learned to sing a song in English. After all these years of imprisonment in one labor camp after another, they were beginning to feel free to be kids again.

Yes, they were free, these children of Poles, Ukrainians, Latvians, Estonians, and Lithuanians, whose parents had been placed in labor camps to do the bidding of the Germans. These were people who had been taken by the Germans to do their hard labor, but the labor camps were different from the concentration camps. Labor camps were for non-Jews, and although people did die in them, they were not set up as death camps. The concentration camps, however, had been reserved mostly for the Jews, and from these no one was ever intended to emerge alive. Many of our DP camp population— and most of the children—were non-Jews from the labor camps, for very few Jews, and almost no Jewish children, had survived.

Now, unlike the Jews, the survivors of the labor camps were free to do what they wanted. Many of them wanted to return to their homelands. Repatriation trains were organized, and day by day trains left Germany taking these people and their children home.

My friend Dorothy Jones accompanied one transport to Poland. I couldn't wait for her return. I longed to hear her impressions of my beloved country. When she finally arrived, I bombarded her with questions: "What did you think? How was it?" She told me about the mountains, about the hills, and then she said, "They have the best apples I have ever tasted." I could almost taste one myself. How well I remembered going to my grandmother's farm and picking apples. I also remembered the mountains and the rivers and my home—the home I lived in with my parents and my sisters and my little brother. The house was in the middle of the village. I knew everybody there. I went to school with all the children who lived in this village and around it. I remembered it so well. As Dorothy was talking I felt a pain in my chest; I had such a longing for it all. I missed my home, my family, and my friends. But I knew that I could never take one of those repatriation trains to Poland, for there was no room for Jews there. We were no longer citizens of Poland. Our orders clearly stated not to send any Jewish people there.

Another trainload left for Poland, and my heart was

heavy when I returned home that day. My sisters were already seated around the table waiting for me, so that they could eat dinner. They tried to talk to me, but I was barely listening. I wanted to be alone. A deep feeling of loneliness had settled in my chest. For a moment I felt as if I was all alone in the world. There was a void, one I felt would never be filled. I had felt this void for a long time, but I never wanted to admit it, not even to myself. I simply didn't want to accept the fact that my parents were gone forever. I couldn't face the truth. After all, I didn't bury them; I didn't live through the final act of losing them. My mind was telling me to accept the fact that they were dead, but my heart couldn't seem to manage the task.

Suddenly, a violent cry shook my body. My sisters surrounded me and tried to calm me, but I didn't even see them. All I could see was the face of my mother, and I could hear the last words she uttered: "My angels, my darlings, do take care of each other." I could see my father's big eyes looking at me with concern, and as if in a fog the small face of my brother passed before my eyes. My hands were stretched out to reach them, to touch them.

My sisters led me to bed and tucked me in; then they left me with my pain. My heart was filled with sorrow. I slept, and in my dream I felt the ache so intensely that I could see the tears rolling down my cheeks, and disappearing somewhere. I saw a box, but where there should have been a jack-in-the-box, I could see only tears. My tears were flowing into the box, and then overflowing. Finally, the flood was so tremendous that the box opened and all the tears that had been hidden there for such a long time came out of the box and into my heart.

9. *It Is Not in My Power to Forgive*

With all this pain in my heart, how could I have survived?
How did my three sisters and I survive? How did anyone
manage to survive? We have been asked these questions
over and over again. I have spent a lifetime asking myself
these questions.

I believe first and foremost that my faith in God made
the difference for me. Maybe it is more accurate to say I "got
religion" in the concentration camps. When the pain was
unbearable, when tortures were beyond description, when
starvation turned my insides out, when fear and loneliness
permeated my whole body and soul, I had to find something,
I had to seek someone to turn to. That is when I found God.
I would pray hard, not the words of prayer that I hardly
remembered, but I would confide in God and tell God all
about my pain and about my fears, and I would place my
soul in His hands. The Lord was the strength of my life. I
would almost find peace knowing that my life was in God's
hands. When I woke up each morning I thanked God again
for keeping me alive and able to face another day. I still thank
God each and every day. I look around me and I see God
everywhere, and I'm not afraid. I'm not afraid to live; I'm
not afraid to die.

I believe that the other thing that helped me to survive
was the fact that I was together with my sisters. True, they
were younger than I, and I took care of them more than the
other way around, but we had such a tremendous bond
between us. Their presence was such a great comfort to me,
and taking care of them was such a great motivation to me to

stay alive. We loved and cared for each other. We were left alone at a very early age, the four of us without a mother or father. We had to learn to take care of ourselves even though nobody had ever prepared us for what we faced with each new day. How *could* anyone have prepared us for the Holocaust? Who in the world would believe that such a catastrophe could happen in the twentieth century in a cultured country like Germany?

Hitler's plan was to wipe the Jews from the face of the earth, but that was not my sisters' and my plan. We were determined to cheat on Hitler. We were determined to survive, and it was this tremendous need to withstand all that was heaped upon us that gave us the strength to face each new, horrifying day. The four of us were so close that sometimes we acted as one. When one sister was dying of starvation, another would take a piece of food from her own mouth and hand it to her. Instead of one brain, we had four. This enabled us to figure out what to do next, how to hide, how to escape the worst. We were lucky that we had each other, and of course, much more so that all four of us survived.

Luck played a great role in our survival. I could not begin to recount the number of times we were destined for the gas chambers, or a mass grave, only to get out at the last moment. Even when we begged to go with our dear mother to the gas chambers of Auschwitz, we were pushed away by the SS guards.

There were also some wonderful people around us who helped us to survive. During the last days of the war, I was in desperate shape. My body refused to obey my commands; my legs couldn't carry me anymore. There was a woman among us—her name, I remember, was Mrs. Tyras—who found some kernels of wheat on the floor of the barn we were in, and shared them with me. This seemingly small gesture saved my life. Mrs. Tyras gave me not only the physical nourishment I needed, but also the emotional strength to continue. It was that very night that my sisters and I hid in the hole in the barn and escaped from the death march into freedom.

We all had to find something to hold onto in order to survive. For some it was the idea of finding a husband, a wife, or a friend. For others it was to be reunited with their parents and families. For some it was simply to be free again. For others yet it was a craving for revenge. Many young men survived the horrors, planning to inflict the same suffering on the Germans. I'll never forget a young Jewish boy who was brought to the hospital a few weeks after the end of the war. He had found a machine gun in the woods and gathered several German soldiers who were still running from the Americans. He lined them up, just as they had done to the Jews, and riddled their bodies with bullets. Suddenly his knees shook, his hands trembled; he lost control and the machine gun shot bullets into his own body. He died shortly after he was brought to us. This young man wanted vengeance, but he couldn't take the sight of the bodies he had killed. He couldn't withstand what his hatred had done to him. He was another victim of hatred and persecution.

My sisters and I knew that we couldn't let hatred and vengeance consume us. We had seen so much of it; we had lived through it, and now was the time to begin a new life. We had to reach for love, for understanding, and we had to find a place where we could finally live in peace.

In the meantime weeks and months went by, and we were still in Germany. We had no choice in the matter. Everywhere we went, every time we walked out of the house, we were surrounded by Germans. In the first few weeks we were all afraid to walk in the streets. In every German we saw a killer, a murderer. We were always aware of someone walking behind us and expected a bullet at each and every corner. As we spent more and more time with the Americans, and as their presence became more apparent, we began to feel more secure. We trusted that they would defend us and wouldn't let anybody do us harm, but it was a difficult transition. In every German face we still saw one of the Nazis who had killed our parents, our brother, and all our relatives and friends. I often thought about what I would do if I actually *did* see one of these Nazis.

One particular face haunted me; he was always in my mind. One night in the camps, the Nazis ordered all the mothers to bring their babies to a certain area. I was awakened by a big man, or so he seemed to me then, trying to pull a baby from a young mother, just outside my window. She fell to the ground, covering her baby with her own body. He reached for his gun and fired a number of bullets into her and her little baby. I will never be able to erase this scene from my mind. The bulging eyes of the SS man will forever haunt me. What would I do if I saw him? Could I reach for a gun and pierce his body with bullets? Or would I run from him in fear? I didn't know; I really didn't know what I would do.

The news of the Nuremberg trials was on the lips of all the survivors. We were all hoping that some justice would be done. But the Germans weren't at all interested in punishing the criminals. After all, they would have to punish all of the German people. The Americans and the British made a circus of the trial. I spent one day at the courthouse and came home absolutely crushed. The judges made it sound as if these people were being tried for stealing a slice of bread or a piece of silver. I could not believe what I was hearing. I knew one of the judges, and after that day I could no longer look him in the eyes. By God, I thought, didn't these people understand? Didn't they know by now that these Nazis were murderers, that they had the blood of one and a half million little children on their hands, as well as the lives of ten and a half million innocent adults?

In my work with UNRRA I came across many German officials. They always tried to apologize, but I couldn't understand what their apologies were supposed to mean to me. I would listen to them say, "We didn't know; we didn't see anything." All I could think of was the time when we were in a camp in the middle of Germany, deep in the country. Gundelsdorf was a small town with a population of about five hundred people. There was a manufacturing plant there, and we had to load trains with some tremendously heavy material. We carried loads, like telephone poles, day in and day out. We had hardly any food, and we were in rags in the middle of winter. We lived in a barrack, hastily erected for us with no heat, no beds, and a hard frozen floor on which we slept. *Everybody* in this small town could see us working and dying, working and dying, for if one of us couldn't perform, she was shot instantly, on the spot, still carrying her extremely heavy load.

One hundred of us women had arrived at Gundelsdorf around Christmas time, the festivity of the holiday in the air. We heard the church bells ringing as people went in to pray and talk to God. How in the world could they face God? At first we were hoping that the townspeople would take over the camp, that they would save us. The trauma of being among "normal" people and not being helped was much more painful than the starvation and the tortures. These people knew what was happening, could see it in plain view, and still they did nothing. Nobody, but nobody, can ever tell me that they didn't know.

Everybody knew. The German people knew—every German alive during this time knew what was happening. And yes, the Americans knew it, too. The whole world knew and did nothing. They did nothing when little children were gassed, when their little heads were smashed against the walls of the ghettos and concentration camps. *They did nothing*. But worst of all, it was done by "nice, cultured, educated Germans." The German people had another excuse: "Hitler did it all." Hitler couldn't have done it alone. Oh, no, my dear, Hitler didn't do it; *you* did it—you and you and you . . . Some days the idea of living among all these Germans whom I knew to be guilty of crimes beyond description depressed me so completely that I would spend the next few days and nights dreaming of escape from their country.

One day my sister Anna came home yelling: "I saw Gips! I saw Gips! I swear I saw him!" Gips was an SS officer in one of the camps where we were imprisoned. He always walked around with a dog whip, and if someone didn't perform to his satisfaction, he would beat them to death. We lived in fear of this man; we shook when we saw him coming. I listened to Anna, and I realized that my worst fear was coming true. But at that moment, I knew that I had to do something. I went to the city clerk and learned where Gips lived. I wasn't sure what I would do when I faced him, or even what I *wanted* to do, but I knew that I had to frighten him, to see him shake.

I asked a friend to go with me to Gips's apartment. I didn't want any of my sisters with me. I was afraid of their reaction and afraid for them. We found the apartment building and walked up three flights of stairs. As I stood at the door, my heart was pounding, my knees shaking. I knocked. A woman opened the door, and we walked in without invitation. In front of me sat a little man with two small children next to him. He looked so small. I couldn't believe that this was the same man who had evoked such fear in us, and yet I recognized him immediately. Without his shining uniform, without his hat, the gun at his side and the whip in his hand, he looked so small. My first instinct was to turn back and run, but I couldn't move. I was glued to the floor. He stood up. He recognized me and the blood drained from his face. He was white, and he was shaking. I could see him trembling. I gathered the courage I knew I had within me. I walked close to him, and I slapped his face back and forth.

"My God," I screamed, "you have children, little children! How will you tell them about all the little children you killed—how will you explain it to them?"

Gips's children started to cry, and I walked out of the room and ran down the stairs as fast as I could. I was so confused, so bewildered. Could it be that all these killers, all these big men, were really just small men—men whose own children were as young as those they had viciously killed? What would they tell their children when they grew up? How would they explain the atrocities, the murders they committed? How could they sleep at night? How could they live with what they had done?

Nothing that I could do to this one SS man would do

justice for all the atrocities he'd committed. I couldn't do anything to him anyhow. Was I right or wrong? Should I have reported him? Should I have killed him? What could I do?

All I know is that the fear remained in my heart for a long time, but not so the hate. I couldn't find any hatred when I looked into my heart. I was trying so hard to forget, to start a new life with love instead of hate, with understanding rather than punishment. I wondered, could it be that I had succeeded in getting over the hell I had lived? Could it be that I had reached a point in my life where I could begin to forgive people, even Germans? I couldn't honestly say. I might be able to live without hate, but I knew that I would never be able to forget. I could never, never forget, and I certainly am not able to forgive. I have no right to forgive. It isn't up to me to exonerate the Germans for the lives of millions of people who were killed, murdered, slaughtered. It is not in my power to forgive.

10. The Love of My Life

This was one of the mornings that I didn't think I could get up and go to work, but my sisters greeted me warmly, and seeing how great they looked, and how much love they showed me, I gained the strength to face the day. I knew that my sisters depended on me, and I knew that I had to be there for them.

All my sisters and I wished for was to be free! We dreamed about it, we talked about it, but the simple fact was that we were still in Germany. We were scared to be there, but we didn't have any other place to go. We dreamed about going to America, the *goldeneh medina*, or "golden land," as our parents had called it in Yiddish. But in the meantime, I was so engrossed in my work that there were days when I thought I would have to stay in Germany until every Allied person, and definitely every Jew, left this country.

My supervisor was now the director of operations for Bavaria (the southern region of Germany), and he promoted me to camp welfare officer for the area. My days were so filled with people and their problems that I hardly had time to think about what might happen to us. I hadn't even noticed that my sisters and the girls who lived with us were getting involved with some young men—some with American soldiers, and others with survivors like ourselves. Young people were reaching out to other young people; the news of seven young girls travelled far and wide, and pretty soon young men were knocking at our door.

I, however, was too busy for a social life. Mr. Milus, with whom I worked closely, noticed this, and took a somewhat paternal interest in introducing me to someone. He wanted to do something nice for me; he appreciated my work and my dedication, and many times mentioned how he admired me for having recovered psychologically, for leaving hatred behind and being able to reach out to people and work to help others recover. Little did he know how difficult it was at times. To build faith in humanity, to discover that there were human beings even among the Germans, to show feelings, to spread love rather than hate, and to have faith in God—these were difficult tasks indeed.

One day Mr. Milus suggested that we take a ride to a small town where he had worked before. There was a whole group of young doctors from Poland there who had opened a hospital for displaced persons. Mr. Milus picked me up on a cold but beautiful Sunday morning. We drove about eighty kilometers (fifty miles) before we reached the small town of Schwandorf. We found the hospital without any difficulty. As soon as we entered, we were greeted by several young men who were very happy to see their former director and who looked me over with curiosity. I was a young, fairly good-looking girl, wearing an army-like uniform, and I spoke their own language, Polish.

It was lunchtime and everybody gathered around the table. After a short introduction, a barrage of questions came from all sides: "Where are you from? Which concentration camps were you in? Have you been in Auschwitz? Where do you live now?" Questions, questions. Mr. Milus was soon completely forgotten, for we survivors had so much in common, and so much to discuss.

One of the doctors, Danek, remembered me from the concentration camp Plaszow. He had treated me for the terrible headaches I suffered. He remembered that I was hospitalized when a number of patients were taken for extermination, but I was saved. He claimed that he had saved me by stating in my records that I was to be released immediately. As he spoke, I began to relive the experience: I could feel the pain and fear that I lived through that day.

The SS walked into the hospital room and took a woman

in the bed next to me. She was expecting a baby at any moment. The SS officer's eyes pierced through me, and then on to the next bed and the next. Several women were removed from their beds. I could feel my knees shaking and my head spinning; I was waiting for him to point his finger at me. But, as if by some miracle, he passed me by and left the room. I could never forget the faces of those young women who were buried on the grounds of the camps that night.

Of course I remembered this young doctor, for being hospitalized in a camp was already a step towards death, and finding someone who was kind and willing to help was indeed a revelation. Danek had done what he could during the war, even though it was not easy. Then, only a few days after the war ended, he and another doctor requisitioned a German casino with the help of the American occupation forces, and they converted it into a hospital—this hospital, where we now sat eating dinner.

Danek and the other doctor had gotten some conscientious American soldiers to bring in army cots and blankets, and even requisition food for the sick; within two weeks these doctors, who had hardly recovered from their own wounds of war and persecution, were running a hospital and giving help to the sick and dying. Many of their patients never lived to experience freedom, but spending their last few days in a warm bed and having some food was also a blessing.

Mr. Milus told me that the two young doctors, Danek and Henry, worked day and night in those early days even though they were as undernourished and exhausted as their patients. One night Henry was shaking. He had chills and fever. His patients had typhus, and in his weakened state he could not fight it. For weeks he had to stay in the hospital as a patient while Danek took care of him. As soon as he was feeling better, he decided to go to Poland to look for his family. He was very devoted to his mother and father, and he had to know whether they were dead or alive.

When I came for this first visit to Schwandorf, Henry was still in Poland looking for his family. During the next two months Danek and I visited each other several times, and a warm friendship developed.

On December 1, 1945, my sisters wanted to go to Schwandorf. They had met some of the men who worked in the hospital, and they really wanted to go without me, without their maminka who chaperoned them all the time; they wanted to have some fun. But I didn't feel right about letting them go alone, and at the last minute I popped into the car and went with them to Schwandorf.

Five young brides-to-be jumped out of the car, and all the young men greeted them with whistles, kisses, and hugs. There was a kind of wildness in these creatures who for six years couldn't touch each other, who had suffered not only starvation, persecution, and diseases, but also the agony of loneliness. Suddenly they were free. They were very young— all in their late teens—but growing up fast. They wanted to kiss, to touch a girl, and perhaps even more, but they had to know their limits. This was all temporary, nothing was permanent, so a lasting relationship couldn't exist, I thought.

Danek was busy at the hospital when we arrived. I spent some time with a doctor who by coincidence was my mother's physician in Krakow before the war. He had just arrived from Poland with his wife. He began to reminisce, and the painful memories of my dear mother and father were touched upon again. When my sisters weren't around, I would speak of Mother and Father; but when they were with me, I avoided it. The wounds were still very raw.

Dinner was prepared by the hospital staff, and we were all invited. It was amazing to my sisters and me that our "family" consisted of women, except for Kurt, and this family was mostly men. Each of us had a male companion. I was paired with Danek but couldn't quite figure out what our relationship was. I liked him and enjoyed his company, but I was not falling in love. He was handsome and pleasant, and very nice to me at a time when I was hungry for affection, starved for men; yet nothing was happening. My heart didn't pound, and I didn't see stars when he touched me.

As we were seated for dinner, a tall, good-looking man

sat at the other end of the table. He was introduced as Dr.
Henry Rubinstein, recently returned from his trip to Poland.
His last name sounded familiar to me, but only for a moment.
The conversation at dinner went from food to travel to
weather to the everyday things we all did, and again back to
our past. No matter how or where the conversation would
start, it always ended back there in our former lives, in the
pits of the concentration camps.

The memories were so embedded in our hearts and minds
that we couldn't forget them, not even for a moment. We
went back to the camps again and again. Sometimes it seemed
we almost wanted to torture ourselves, to punish ourselves
for staying alive, for not dying with all the others. Neither
time nor anything else could erase those painful memories.

After dinner, Dr. Rubinstein moved over and began to
quiz me: "Which camps were you in? Where were you
liberated? Have you been in Plaszow?" I nodded, and he
asked: "Did you by any chance meet my mother? She was
working at Madritsch. I heard she was there for a long time.
Perhaps she was in another barrack," he ventured as I shook
my head. "I hear," he continued, "that you were shipped to
Auschwitz in September 1944. I heard she was, too. Are you
sure you didn't know her?" He proceeded to describe her,
how she looked and how she walked. He told me she was the
greatest mother in the world.

My mind was racing as I tried to answer his questions.
My God, six thousand women were shipped from Plaszow to
Auschwitz in cattle cars; how could I remember anyone? I
was with my mother and my three sisters, and we had enough
of a problem trying to stay together and alive under the most
inhuman conditions; who would notice anyone else? I did
remember, however, that there was a segregation as we emptied out of the cattle cars, and many people were taken away
from us. I remembered a dear old woman who had told me
stories about her son the doctor, and who wanted me to
marry him. The Nazis had told her that her son had been
killed in Auschwitz—they had even delivered his ashes to her
in a box—but she refused to believe it. On the way to

Auschwitz, she even talked about how she was going to be reunited with him there. As the SS men pushed her away from us, she turned back and cried out to me, "Please take care of my son!"

But this couldn't be *that* son, the doctor. After all, he had died in Auschwitz years ago . . . hadn't he?

Henry told me about his trip to Poland and how he had met survivors who said they'd heard that his mother went to the gas chambers of Auschwitz and his father also, but he wouldn't believe it until he found someone who at least was there when it happened. Before we left that night, he asked me whether there was a displaced persons' hospital in Tirschenreuth where I worked.

"Yes, of course," I told him, "we have a DP hospital which UNRRA took over from the Germans. The chief medical officer is a Cuban doctor, very young, very talented; he runs the hospital."

"Do you think I could get a job?" he asked. I was surprised, but promised him I'd look into it immediately. In the meantime, I looked into his eyes, and I liked what I saw. He had a very persistent stare which seemed to engulf all of me. He also put his hand on mine as we talked, and his touch sent chills through my body. After I left, this young doctor, who had just met me for the first time in his life, said to his friend Danek: "I think I'll marry that girl."

On our way home the girls were bubbly and giggling, exchanging their experiences with the guys. Anna wanted to know who the guy was who had kept his eye on me all through dinner. Dear Anna, she always spied on me. I could picture her telling our mother that this boy or another had kissed me; she was always behind me wanting to know what the boys were telling me. She was my shadow.

I mentioned that this young doctor had asked me about his mother and wanted to know whether we had seen her in Plaszow or in Auschwitz. Before I even finished telling them about it, Anna had an answer, she knew it right away: "Of course," she yelled, "that was his mother, you know, the one who wanted you to marry her beautiful son, the doctor, that funny kid photographed in his high school uniform. That funny kid must be him! My God, are you going to marry him? I don't believe it! That must be him, but he turned out all right. He doesn't look anything like the crazy kid in her picture, or a dead one whose ashes came from Auschwitz, remember? He doesn't look dead to me; he seems very much alive, and very much after you. I could see it, I swear!"

There was no way to stop Anna once she got started. I tried to interrupt her; I didn't want to hear any of it. I was scared and bewildered. Pola, Anna, Mania, and Gienia screamed, laughed, and yelled: "You are going to marry him! You are going to marry him! He is a doctor; he will cure us all! He'll marry our maminka. What shall we call him—Papinka?" and on they went.

"Now, hold your horses!" I yelled. "I'm not marrying anybody, by God—I just met this man."

"But his mother said you'd marry her son; you must."

"Please, you sillies, will you just forget it? So, I knew his mother, so she wanted me to marry him. She is dead now, and it was a long time ago, and it doesn't mean a thing now," I blurted.

"If you say so," my sisters said grudgingly.

There was silence for a moment, and then Pola started up again: "I can't wait to tell him about his father. Remember, he wouldn't let me use his iron. I wanted to boil some water on it, and he grumbled, 'It's for ironing and not for boiling water.' He ironed uniforms at Madritsch, and I guess he was frightened that he might get caught letting us use it. How much good did it do him? He was one of the first to go to Auschwitz. He went with a group of older men."

"Wait till he hears about his mother, " Mania continued. "God, did she love him! Remember the sanitation control, how they made you take off all your clothes, and then they searched you to see if you were hiding any valuables. I don't know how she managed to come out of there with his picture, but she did. How she talked about him; she thought he was God. Oh my, did she exaggerate!

81

"Didn't she teach you how to cook his favorite dishes? Oh, boy, you have it made. Isn't that the way to a man, through his stomach? You know all his favorite dishes—that's great!" Mania laughed and all the girls burst out laughing and giggling.

"Listen, you; listen, that's enough!" I yelled. "Not a word out of any of you! I don't want to talk about it, and I don't want you to tell him any of it! Not a peep out of you! Perhaps the time will come when I may decide to tell him about his mother and father, but I'll make that decision and only I! Understood?" I made my statement very clearly. I didn't want Henry to know about his mother's wishes. I was suddenly scared. What if . . . ? But no, I didn't even want to think about it.

I didn't sleep that night. I went to work the next morning utterly exhausted. At midday the telephone rang. "This is Henry," I heard at the other end of the line.

I swallowed hard. "Where are you calling from?" I asked.

"I'm right here at the post office."

"You mean in Tirschenreuth?" I stammered.

"May I come over?"

"Yes, of course, it's only a block away," I explained, reaching for my skirt, for my hair. I didn't know which to straighten out first. I had to fix my hair. I had to do something. I had to look good. But why? I moved automatically, even trying to clean off my desk. When he walked in, my face was flushed, and I could hear my heart pounding in my ears. My God, I had seen men before. Why all the excitement about this one?

After a short greeting he asked me if I could show him the hospital. Since it was my lunch break, I called the head doctor and asked if he could have lunch with us. Dr. Vallejo was a jolly man. He had just finished his medical training and wanted to operate on every appendix, set of tonsils, uterus, anything that would come under his knife. He was a good surgeon and a very warm human being. He certainly could use some help in the hospital. Before we finished our lunch Henry had a job in the DP hospital in Tirschenreuth under

UNRRA Team 168. After work I went with him to look at some apartments in town, and when he left for Schwandorf that evening he had a new job, a place to live, and plans to move the following week.

I couldn't quite comprehend how and why it all happened, but as soon as he moved in he asked me for a date, and then another, and another. We met almost every night. We took long walks, and we talked and talked. We enjoyed nature; we listened to the birds singing; we loved holding hands and just celebrating being alive. When we came to my house, we found six giggling females and fourteen-year-old Kurt, who by now was as much a part of the family as anybody else. The girls prepared delicious meals, and my young doctor delighted in the feast and even more in the wonderfully warm, family-like ambiance that surrounded him.

Kurt was the only man in our family until Henry came along, and Kurt didn't like this intrusion. He sulked when Henry came over and he kept telling me, "Maminka, don't marry this guy; he only wants your money." He didn't want another man in the house. This overgrown man of fourteen!

A man in the house . . . I couldn't think about another man in the house, either. How many miracles had we sisters performed to stay together, to survive? Nobody could come between us now. I could already see the fear in my sisters' eyes. I could see their resistance towards Henry and the cold shoulder he would get every time he tried to get closer to them. When I first met Henry they were so excited about him, I thought they would embrace him and welcome him into the family; but the closer he and I got, the more they pulled away from him. He was a stranger, older than any of us, and a professional; my sisters seemed to feel that he was an outsider who would take away their maminka and separate them all.

I lay awake at night trying to figure it all out. But when I was alone with him and he held my hand or kissed me, I felt I wanted more and more. I wanted to be with him, to be near him. God! Did I need that! I knew I was getting close to him, but not close enough to have any erotic feelings. I felt warmth when he touched me, but no sexual desire. I couldn't understand this. I thought that now that I was free, now that the war was over, I should have normal feelings. I should have a desire for sex. But I didn't feel anything. My menstruation hadn't come back yet, and I thought that maybe this was why my feelings were deadened: my hormones weren't working properly.

I gathered all my courage and went to see a doctor one day. I couldn't go to the UNRRA hospital for fear Henry would find out about my problem, so I had no choice but to see a German doctor. My fear was so powerful that I almost turned back from the waiting room and ran home, but I had to know. I had to know whether there was any hope for me. The doctor examined me carefully. I kept my eyes closed throughout the whole procedure. When it was all over, I took a deep breath to make sure I was still alive. There was nothing wrong with me, the doctor assured me, and he thought that my menstruation should come back soon.

My job took me away on trips, and every time I was away I dreamed about coming back home. I longed to be back, and not so much with my sisters, but with my new friend. Even when I was many miles away I could feel his presence. I longed to touch him, to be touched, and to be near him. When I returned from one long trip, he told me how much he had missed me and how much he needed me, and simply said: "Let's get married." This was only five weeks after we met. The rush scared me. There was no war anymore. We had a lifetime ahead of us; why rush? Or was it perhaps because we were still afraid? Afraid to be separated? Afraid to be alone? Before I could open my mouth, he rushed into the kitchen and told the girls: "We're getting married; your maminka and I are getting married!" I remember my sisters' faces, their mouths open. But he didn't give them any time to react, either. He kissed them all and bubbled, "I'm getting married to your maminka," and he whirled me around and kissed me passionately in front of everyone.

On January 20, 1946, we had an engagement party. I

arranged a beautiful wedding party on the same day for our friend Lola, who had stayed with us since liberation. A wonderful young man who had survived the concentration camps came from Poland looking for a bride. He met Lola and they immediately developed a close relationship. She came from the same part of Poland as he did, and they had had similar upbringings. They were also both religious. Since I was the maminka, he asked me for her hand and even brought me a beautiful basket of flowers. Our dear friend Rabbi Eugene Lipman, who had liberated us, drove from Regensburg to marry Lola and Derek in a lovely ceremony attended by all our friends.

After we were engaged I visited Henry's room more and more often. We longed to be alone. I could feel how much he wanted me, but I believed that this should be postponed until we were married. But one day it happened. He caressed me, kissed me, and I felt a burning desire in me. I was so scared. But when it finally happened I didn't feel anything inside. I felt pain, and I was aware that something had happened to me, but where were the stars? I wondered. Where was the ultimate joy? Why didn't I feel anything wonderful? I knew I couldn't admit this to him, so I pretended to be exhausted, turned over and went to sleep. He awakened me with tender kisses. When I returned home, I felt that everybody knew what had transpired. They all looked at me so strangely, or at least I thought they did.

The next day Henry came to dinner, and after the meal we were going to take a walk. I decided to tell him about his mother. Night after night I dreamed about her; I could see her vividly. She wanted to be a part of this; after all, she had arranged this meeting. The thought of it still scared me. Was it real? Was I doing it for her sake? Was I going to marry him because she wanted me to? These thoughts and many more whirled through my head as I lay awake night after night struggling with what to do. Finally I knew I had to tell him the whole truth.

We were almost finished with dinner when Anna brought up the subject that was so much on my mind: "Did you say your mother was in Plaszow? Didn't you say that you were in Auschwitz for a long time? Your ashes were supposedly sent to your parents?"

"How did you know that?" Henry asked, his face ashen.

"Well," I thought, "here goes . . . ," and the whole story came tumbling out of my mouth. I told him how his mother worked together with us in Madritsch. How she helped me to sew. How she taught me to cook, even though we never had any food—she would pretend so she could show me how to make the dishes Henry liked. How she wanted me to be her daughter-in-law. How she went to Auschwitz in the cattle cars with us, surviving this unbelievable journey, and all along hoping that she would see her only son in Auschwitz, even though his ashes had been sent to her. How she was gassed together with my mother. And what her last words to me were: "Take care of my son."

We went on telling him this unbelievable story, and he sat there tongue-tied and shocked. I kissed him tenderly and told him: "Now you know the whole story. I didn't want to tell you sooner, and I suppose you know why, but I had to tell you now. She loved you so much." He left our house that night with a heavy heart and tears in his eyes. I stayed home. My mind wandered back to the time I was with his mother and then to now, to him, my Henry. Was it a miracle? Was it destiny? What was happening to us? My night was filled with strange dreams.

The days passed quickly. My office was filled with people. Their needs were great and my responsibilities grew with each day. At home things were changing. Lola was married and left our family home. Stella was engaged and would soon be leaving us, too. My sisters all found some young men to keep them busy. I found the atmosphere much easier. I felt less guilty about being with Henry, and we were getting closer with each passing day. Our love deepened, and the preparations for our wedding were underway.

The invitations were printed: "Mania, Pola, and Anna announce the marriage of their sister Ruth to Dr. Henry S. Rubinstein, on March 19, 1946 in Tirschenreuth, Germany."

The names of our parents were missing for our parents were all dead, killed by the Nazis. They were not there to witness this happy union; they were not there to bless us. We did, however, have a lot of friends at the wedding. People from twenty different countries who were working with me at UNRRA joined us in the celebration.

Henry and I were married by Rabbi Lipman, among 250 friends and family members. I can say we danced all night; we did indeed. We did the Polish dances, we did the Jewish dances, we did the Cuban dances and the Russian dances. We even did the German dances, for the *Bürgermeister* (mayor) had given us the place and the orchestra for our wedding. The war was over, we were free, and we wanted to rejoice with all the people of the world. They all wanted to celebrate this marriage ceremony in their own way, and we went along until our feet couldn't carry us anymore. Just before sunrise, Henry and I slipped out, dying to be together, alone and together, showered in kisses and a feeling of oneness that will never be forgotten.

11. Henry's Story: I Must Survive!

It seemed like every day I learned something new. I learned about people, about their feelings and their needs. One day I realized that I wanted to learn more about Henry. I wanted to know about his life before the war, perhaps something about the years in concentration camps. I knew he had been in Auschwitz—the tattoo on his arm made that clear. Mostly I wanted to know how he had managed to survive.

This was one of the rare evenings when I came home and found my sisters out and Henry waiting for me. I rounded up something to eat for dinner, and we took our meal out to the garden. I broached the subject gently: "Now, listen, my love, you've heard my story many times, but I don't know anything about yours. Please tell me, what was it like for you? How did you get out of hell?"

It seemed like Henry had been waiting for this moment. He looked at me questioningly. "You mean, you really want to hear my story?" I nodded and he said, "How about if I tell you what happened at the end of the war. I don't think I can go back into the hell yet." I gave him a hug and he proceeded.

* * *

I was on the death march through the woods in the northern part of Bavaria. We were watched and surrounded by the SS guards and had to go day and night without food or sleep. Many nights we were herded into the woods. It was often raining, or even snowing, and we were literally freezing to death. We had no roof over our heads, and we had nothing but the blue and white striped uniforms to cover our bodies, not even underwear, and certainly no blankets. During the march the guards kept an eye on us constantly, and when someone tried to run away, they would shoot him. Most of us were too frail to run by that point anyway. I always thought about running, though. I would dream of making my escape, even though I didn't have the strength, even though I knew that to run would mean instant death.

Suddenly, one morning, we saw American tanks. As we came closer, the German guards dropped their guns and ran into the woods. We couldn't run after them. We wanted to kill them for what they had done to us, but we didn't have the strength or energy to do anything but stand there and cheer on the American Army. The Americans started shooting at the SS guards, and we were so happy to have the shots aimed at the Germans instead of at us, for a change.

When I saw the Americans. my heart beat so fast I was afraid it would burst. None of us could believe that we had lived to see the Americans, that we had lived to see the end of the war. We wanted to touch them, to see if they were real, but they didn't have time to bother with us. There were still many German units in the woods, and they had to reach them so they could finish this terrible war. As they passed us—thousands of shrivelled men still marching, or rather moving—they threw some food to us, and we grabbed all we could.

This was April 1945. The weather was unbearable. Many people had already died during the march. Those who were unable to walk or who tried to run away were taken into the woods and shot by the German guards. The rest of us had still been following the guards, hoping and praying that the end would come soon. When we saw the first Americans, we thought the end of our suffering had come. But they just marched by us, as soldiers would, and left us alone. Our dreams were shattered; we were devastated and didn't know what to do or what to expect.

The next day we walked into a village, but there was nobody there. The Germans had all run away before the

Americans came. We rushed into the empty homes and grabbed all the food we could find. We had been starving for so long, the sight of food made us wild. We started eating, grabbing and gulping whatever we could get our hands on. But our stomachs couldn't digest the food and most of us got very sick. Many got diarrhea, and within twenty-four hours they were dead of dehydration. They survived the war, but they didn't live to reach freedom.

I ate some food, but I took most of it with me because my stomach was hurting, and I realized the danger of eating. Since we didn't know what to do or where to go, we went on marching through empty villages even though nobody was forcing us to march. I couldn't imagine being anything but an inmate of the concentration camps; I certainly couldn't conceive of being free. I couldn't visualize my life without the guards watching my every move.

On the third of May, 1945, we reached the small town of Schwandorf. We couldn't walk another step. There were only a few hundred of us left, most of us nothing more than walking dead. I still had the little bit of food I had grabbed in that first empty village, and this I forced myself to eat very slowly. I could still walk, which was a miracle. As I sat there after my meal, another miracle happened: my brain began to work again. I could think! I began to plan. I surrounded myself with a few men who couldn't walk anymore and tried to explain to them that if they could only make the last effort and walk with me, I would find a hospital, and I could help them because I was a doctor.

During my imprisonment I had almost forgotten that I was a physician. Many, many years before, I had graduated from medical school in Prague, Czechoslovakia. I had to go there because there was a quota for Jewish students in Poland. I had been lucky: I got into the German university in Prague. I had to study in German and in Czech, but I didn't mind, because I wanted to be a doctor more than anything else. Just before the war I started working in the hospital in Krakow, and then in the ghetto hospital. But in the camps the Germans would never let me work as a doctor; the best I could do was wash the floors in hospitals and serve as an orderly. I always tried to help friends, though. I remember one time I had to operate on a friend using a kitchen knife. I saved his life. There was another man who almost lost his eye, but I saved it.

I thought once a doctor, always a doctor, although the Germans didn't agree with me. I was one of the first taken to Auschwitz, because they wanted to kill all the Jewish professionals. They wanted to break the Jewish community and kill the community leaders, the people others would depend on. It was only through so many miracles, thanks to God, to whom I always turn, that I survived and that I'm still a physician. *Physician, thou shalt heal*—I felt it now with all my heart and soul. I had to help the sick.

I found a hospital run by German nuns. They wouldn't accommodate any of the survivors. For them the war against the Jews was still on. The Americans had already occupied Schwandorf, and I met an American soldier on the street who led me to the American headquarters. They had a German interpreter, and I explained to her that we had to have a hospital. People were dying in the streets, and we had to help them. I explained that I was a doctor, but I could do nothing without a facility. Next to the American office was a casino, a large building. I asked the Americans to requisition it for us to make a temporary hospital. The next day we got the building. I found another doctor among the survivors—Danek—and together we started to organize a hospital. We called it the Casino Hospital. We received some beds and sheets by requisition from the German hospital, but we couldn't get any medications, because they didn't really have any.

Danek and I carried the sick and half dead in our arms, and together we brought about a hundred of them into the hospital. We approached the Americans and the German mayor, and pretty soon we received some physical help and also some medicines. Unfortunately, the medical supplies were very limited. It was just about the time when penicillin came out, but the Americans hardly had enough for their own soldiers. The most important thing was that they were able to help us with food. They gave us some of theirs, and they also requisitioned food for us from the Germans.

My work occupied all of my time, and trying to help these people to survive became a part of my own survival. All I could think of was that we *must* survive. *I must survive!* I didn't even think of my family, my parents, my friends. My whole being was tied up in surviving. Unfortunately, though, people were still dying, and about three weeks later I too was infected with the dreaded disease: typhus. I might have gotten it from the patients, or maybe from the water. The fact is that I contracted it and had a very complicated case. My friend Danek took good care of me. I also believe that my strong will to survive saved my life. After a few weeks, when I was recovered, Danek told me I was well enough to run the hospital by myself, and he went to Poland to look for his family. He returned a few weeks later with his younger brother. They were all that was left of what had once been a large family.

Encouraged by my friend's success in finding his brother, I decided to go to Poland to look for my own family. I couldn't imagine that anyone had survived; I had seen first hand what the Germans did to older people. But I went anyway; I had to know for sure. When I finally arrived in Krakow, where we lived before the war, I searched everywhere and asked everyone about my parents. Some people told me that my mother and father were killed in Auschwitz, but I didn't want to believe it. I found out from others about the death of my aunts and uncles. The only one left from my family was a cousin, also named Henry. He had changed his name and pretended to be Catholic. A woman who worked for his mother had hidden him through the most difficult times. He was overjoyed to see me, but he decided to stay in Krakow. I myself wasn't sure yet what I wanted to do.

I went to see my father's business, and I was hoping to get some money from the people who had taken it over, but they wouldn't hear of it. The Poles had taken over all the Jewish businesses when the Jews were taken away, and now they wouldn't give any of it back. They had stolen my father's business, the house we lived in, and everything in it. I was angry and disappointed. But I was so glad I was alive and that I could walk the streets of my city—something I never imagined I would do again—that my anger changed into joy. I walked for hours, with my memories of days gone by, of the years I had lived there with my sister, my parents, and all my friends.

At first I was so excited to be in my hometown that I even looked into the possibility of working at a hospital in Krakow. One of my cellmates in the concentration camp was Joseph Cyrankiewicz, who became a cabinet minister under the first president of Poland after the war. I wrote to him, and he offered me all the help he could give.

One night I had a terrible dream. I opened my eyes and realized that I was all alone. There was nobody left in Poland. My parents were gone, my friends all dead. It wasn't like home anymore. It was not a place for me to start a new life. I was aware of the fact that even now, after the war, the Polish people were still as antisemitic as ever. There were uprisings against the Jews in several cities in Poland. I thought about all the Polish people who had collaborated with the Nazis, and I was frightened.

The sun had risen, but it was a cold day in Krakow on November 25, 1945. My body shivered, my mind was restless, but I had reached a decision. For better or for worse, I'd return to Germany, and from there I'd try to emigrate to the United States, or to Palestine, or anywhere they would take me.

I was still basically at the stage where my only desires were to have enough food, to have some clothes, not to feel cold, and to be surrounded by people who wouldn't hate me and who didn't want to hurt me. Freedom was still a faraway dream. I couldn't even analyze it; I couldn't imagine being free. As long as the people around me couldn't constantly shoot at me, and wouldn't kill me, as long as I could move freely from one place to another with no electric fence surrounding me, I wanted to keep moving. I wanted to shout for joy; I wanted to live!

On my way back to Germany I stopped in Prague. I found the university and in a couple of days I was able to get a copy of my diploma. With this in hand, I felt like I could conquer the world. I had a quick trip back to Schwandorf, getting rides from Americans whenever possible, climbing aboard trains for the rest. When I reached Schwandorf, I found everything as before. I started to work with all the energy I could gather. I felt safe among the people I was working with, because they all came from the same place I did. My patients were all survivors of the German concentration camps, and they felt safe with me. For me it was a challenge to make them well, to help them recover, because I knew best what they had lived through.

I didn't pay much attention to the Germans. They were in civilian clothing, and I wasn't afraid of them. I hardly had any contact with them, except for the officials who supported the Casino Hospital, and the nurses and other help who worked there. I lived at the hospital, I worked there, and I didn't socialize with anyone from the outside, until I met you.

*　　*　　*

"I must admit," Henry told me, "that the day I met you was the beginning of my real life. I slowly began to take off the shield I had carried all through the war and began to realize that the war was over. I started to breathe freely and took the first steps to life. Week by week my body began to shape; my hair started to grow and my mind began the search for freedom. I love you with all my heart and soul." With this he finished and the two of us found our warm bed and cuddled together for a good night's sleep.

The author, called "Ruth" in this book,
at age three in Poland.

Aaron and Lenore Ferber, the author's parents, with children Ruth, Mania, and Pola in 1929.

Aaron Ferber with children from (top) Mania, Pola, Moshe, and Anna on the river in Jelesnia, Poland, in 1936.

After escaping from the "Death March" in 1945, Ruth and her sisters fled to Czechoslovakia. This picture, taken later that year, shows them as still thin from starvation, with hair only recently grown back. From left: Ruth, Mania, Pola, Anna.

Wedding picture of Ruth and Dr. Henry Rubinstein, March 19, 1946, Tirschenreuth, Germany. The invitation was issued by Ruth's sisters, as both their parents had been killed in the Holocaust. Over 250 friends from twenty countries attended the wedding.

Kurt, just before emigration to England where his mother waited for him. She had been located by Ruth through an uncle in Argentina. From left: friends Bronia and Lola, Kurt, Ruth, Anna, and Gienia.

Rabbi Eugene Lipman, a U.S. Army chaplain, was stationed at Susice, Czechoslovakia, when he met Ruth and her sisters and gave them their first real meal in six years. He risked court-martial by arranging illegal transports of Jews to Palestine after the war. He was a close friend until his death in 1994.

The United Nations Relief and Rehabilitation Administration (UNRRA) was formed in 1945 to help displaced persons with the staggering problems of dislocation, homelessness, joblessness, and emotional and physical damage. Ruth (seated lower left, top) was hired for team 168 because of her language abilities. She took special interest in the few surviving children, for whom she started a school (see below).

Miss E. Rubinstein our kind and careful guardian of children, we thank very very much in the name of camp residents and wish a really HAPPY NEW YEAR

FROM RAITERSACH

1948

Anna (left) and Mania, Stuttgart, Germany, 1947. The youngest Ferber sister, Anna was nine years old when the war started. She survived Auschwitz in part by trying to look older and performing very hard labor. Mania, at age twenty-two after the war, had always believed that the sisters would survive.

Pola and Dolek on their wedding day. On the "Death March" Pola had spotted the hiding place under the barn; her quick wits saved the sisters and their friend, Gienia. She was seventeen years old at the time.

Ruth and Henry's first child Ellen, at age three-and-a-half. Her death from leukemia just months after her fourth birthday in 1952 was a crushing blow to the young parents, who had come to America to build a new life.

Ruth and Henry, Erlangen, Germany, 1948. All Ruth's sisters had already emigrated by the time the Rubinsteins' papers came, but Henry's lungs had been damaged in Auschwitz and the couple was refused clearance. After almost five years working for UNRRA and helping thousands of emigrants, Ruth took the matter into her own hands: A second set of X-rays cleared Henry, and they embarked for America with their daughter Ellen on December 1, 1949.

12. New Beginnings, New Lives

I was so involved with Henry and my new life that sometimes I felt guilty about not spending enough time with my sisters. We were all still living in the same house; at dinner time, we sat around the table and the conversation went from the day-to-day problems into everyone's private lives. At times, I noticed that Henry would leave the table; it must have been too much for him to deal with the personal tribulations of all my sisters. But I was their maminka; I always tried to listen to their troubles and share in what they were doing.

Once in a while, I would take a day off from work in order to give all my attention to my sisters. On one such day, I had the UNRRA chauffeur drive me and Mania out of town, to a beautiful place on the river, to spend a little time alone together. I thought I knew everything about her life, but she shared some things with me that I had not known before. She told me how scared she had been all the time when I first started working after the war. She was too timid even to venture out of the house alone. One day, after we had moved to Tirschenreuth, some American soldiers had come to visit my sisters while I was away at work. One young man in particular had taken a liking to Mania, and he tried to kiss her. The poor girl was terrified; she didn't know anything about sex, and she thought that she could get pregnant by kissing. The soldier was amazed at Mania's innocence, but she wouldn't let him touch her. This was her first experience with a man, and she told me that right then and there she had vowed she would never let a man near her until she was married.

Mania and I laughed a little over her naiveté, but underneath our laughter there was sadness, for we both knew the reason why she had been so uninformed. She had been only fourteen years old when the war started, and she never got a chance to have a mother-daughter chat on the subject of the facts of life. The normal rituals of adolescence had been obliterated for her by six years of hard labor, starvation, and loss in the Nazi death camps.

Our conversation turned deadly serious, and Mania told me tearfully that she believed it was only our staying together throughout the war that had kept us alive. We had always shared our last drop of water or crumb of bread; we had supported each other physically and morally. We hugged each other and cried together, and then she wiped her eyes and told me that all that mattered was that we sisters were alive and together. "You are married now," she said, "and it is different having a man in the house, but we all love Henry and he is one of us." These words were music to my ears, and we rode home together in high spirits.

My marriage was not the only change that was going on in our little household. Now Kurt's life was about to take an exciting turn as well. One day I was sitting in my office sorting through the mail, when I came across a letter addressed to me, from England. As I opened it a picture of a beautiful woman slid onto my desk. I looked at the picture, but it was nobody I knew. I turned it over, and the inscription read: "*Meinen lieben Kurt, deine Mutti*" ("To my dear Kurt, from your mother"). I read the letter rapidly and sent a courier on a motorcycle to fetch Kurt and bring him to my office. I had to see his face when he read the letter. I was so excited and happy for him.

It turned out that Kurt's uncle Speiser had received my letter through the Jewish Community Center in Buenos Aires, and he knew that his sister, Kurt's mother, had survived and now lived in England. To save time he wrote directly to her, and she immediately answered through the army post office address I had given.

I'll never forget how Kurt held the picture of his mother,

kissing it and whispering over and over again, "Mutti, Mutti, my Mutti." I started the emigration procedures immediately. The paperwork was ponderous; Kurt had to obtain an affidavit from his mother, stating that she would indeed take care of him, and that he would not be a burden to the state. Meanwhile, during all the bureaucratic processing, Kurt had to go live in a children's center for three months. He found it very difficult to part with us, his surrogate family, and a few times he left the center and tried to walk the hundreds of miles to Tirschenreuth. All the stress was eventually worth it, though, for in July 1946, six months after his mother's letter had arrived, Kurt was reunited with her in London. He wrote me a letter, saying, "I found my real mother, thanks to you, but you'll always be my maminka."

Good things were happening for Pola these days, too. One day a young man came into my office and asked about finding place to stay while he was waiting to emigrate to the U.S. He drove into the city on a motorcycle, dressed in a nice leather coat. I found a place for him, and asked Pola, who was working in my office at the time, to show him the way. She climbed on his motorcycle, and it was love at first sight. They soon became constant companions. Dolek already had papers to go to America, and he wanted Pola to go with him, but she felt she couldn't leave us, her sisters. We were so bound together that separation seemed impossible. Dolek loved her enough to delay his emigration, and the two decided to stay in Tirschenreuth for a while and get married.

Since there were a couple hundred survivors in our little town, a small synagogue had been built, and Pola and Dolek were married there in October 1946. Rabbi Lipman once again came to town from his post in Regensburg to perform the ceremony. It was a traditional wedding according to the Jewish religion. I was so happy that they wanted a traditional wedding; so many times, Pola had expressed her doubts about having faith in God. "Where was God when the little children were killed?" she would say. But through Dolek, she seemed to have regained some of her lost faith. She told me that although it was sometimes difficult to believe in God after all we had been through, she and Dolek felt very strongly that they must forever continue the Jewish tradition that the Nazis had tried to destroy. Pola said that to celebrate her marriage without our parents and without our little brother was very sad, but she and Dolek felt they had to go on, to hold onto their Jewish heritage and to build a better future for themselves and for their children.

Dolek was trained as a dentist, and he managed to get a job in town. It was enough to put food on their table, and they were slowly establishing a normal life, or at least, as normal as life could be living in Germany, surrounded by our enemies. Pola still felt afraid to live among the Germans, but for now it was the best we all could do.

While I was settling into my new marriage, Kurt was being reunited with his mother, and Pola and Dolek were starting their new life together, Gienia was consumed with thoughts of looking for her family. She had been one of ten children, and she wondered if anyone might still be alive somewhere. Finally, she went to Poland to search for them and to find out once and for all the fate of her loved ones. She walked the streets of Krakow, frightened to death. Finally she worked up the courage to knock at the door of her family home. A Polish family was living there, and they told her that no one from her family had returned from the war. Gienia went to the office where Jewish survivors were listed, and she learned that one of her sisters and a brother had survived and were now in Palestine. The Polish people that Gienia had contact with all urged her to leave Poland. She had a strong feeling that the Poles did not want the Jews back—that they, like the Germans, wanted to be rid of the Jews. Feeling unwelcome and alienated, she decided to return to us in Tirschenreuth. Germany was no paradise, but at least she knew she would be among friends.

During Gienia's absence, a new member had been added to our extended family. My uncle Jack, the youngest of my father's eight brothers, had survived the war and was looking all over for family. His search had led him to us in Tirschenreuth. Through my connections with UNRRA, I was able to get him a nice room in the Bahnhoff Hotel, where a number of other survivors lived, and we now spent many evenings together as a family, getting to know each other again and sharing our experiences. Gienia and Jack felt an immediate connection. Indeed, Gienia later told me that the day she returned from Poland and met my uncle Jack was the luckiest day of her life. The two were to be married just six months later, and Gienia, to whom I was maminka, became my aunt!

13. "Wouldn't the World Embrace Us?"

In January 1947 I was transferred to Erlangen, as a sub-area child care officer. Erlangen was a university town in Bavaria, the southern part of Germany. It was near Nuremberg. Henry and I were given a beautiful home from which a Nazi doctor had been evacuated. The house had a swimming pool and a lovely garden. I loved living there, but I missed my sisters terribly.

Henry and I didn't have much time together now either. My office was filled with young people from morning until evening; I often stayed at work until long after dark trying to help them. Strangely enough I was now dealing with many Jewish girls and boys. They were all seeking some way to pursue their education, which they had been forced to stop before the war. They wanted to go to college, but none of them had any papers stating that they had graduated from high school. Indeed many of them never had, but were eighteen years or older. I established a relationship with the university administration and succeeded in getting quite a few of them into the University of Erlangen. They made diligent students, working day and night to achieve their goals despite the odds against them. I was very proud.

Another difficult situation I had to attend to was the people in mental institutions. Due to language difficulty, or simply an attitude of indifference, many displaced persons who were not mentally ill had been committed, some of them for years. One day, I brought a UN doctor to the hospital with me. At one psychiatric hospital we talked to the women who were imprisoned there. Suddenly during the rounds, a woman from Poland started screaming at me and hitting me. "You're Jewish, aren't you?" she yelled in Polish. "I know you are. You killed Christ; I know you did."

The poor UN doctor didn't know whose rescue to go to.

"How come Hitler didn't kill you all? You have no right to be on this earth!" the woman railed.

I tried to touch her, but she wouldn't let me. I was so sad for her.

During the following months, I made many more visits to this hospital with the UN doctor, and we saw to it that those patients who were not mentally ill were repatriated to their homelands. This was a very painful and difficult time for all of us.

My work with the United Nations team in Erlangen continued. People from twenty countries around the world worked with me. We worked well together. We understood each other's pain and joy. After this unbelievable chapter in human history when men killed one another for the sake of killing, when one man and his people decided to wipe another people from the face of the earth, it became our mission to prove that human beings could live together and work together. We all strove for everlasting peace. It was what we dreamed of on those miserable, sleepless nights when we were haunted by the faces of the suffering; we were determined not to be disappointed.

Germany was under the American occupation, and each city was ruled by an American governor. The governor of the city of Erlangen was Col. Frederick Robie, who had been secretary of state in Maine, before the war. Colonel Robie and his wife, Alice, were the most outstanding people I had ever met. I would sit with the colonel for hours and listen to stories of his family coming to America from England in the early days. He told me about life in America at the turn of the century, and all about his family's history, but he never probed into my life in the concentration camps, even though he was doing an in-depth investigation of Nazi war actions. He understood how it hurt, how fresh the wounds were, and he respected my feelings.

The Robies informally adopted Henry and me, for we no longer had any parents. I learned more from my adopted grandmother Alice than I can adequately put into words. She, like my own grandmother many years before, would help the sick and the poor. She would arrange wedding parties for young people who couldn't afford it. She was at the side of the sick at the hospital, trying to comfort them. She sent food to the poor and gave strength to the weak.

And I also learned many practical things from Grandma Robie. I learned how to entertain people without being nervous, how to cook and how to serve. She even taught me to arrange flowers. But most of all I learned about life. I learned that we can all love each other and live with one another. I learned that people are not really different, and that being Jewish didn't make me freaky, or someone to be hated and despised, but that as a Jew, I could be respected by others, just as I could respect other people of different races and religions. I learned that human values are what is important, and that I could honor my tradition and religion, and still be a good citizen of the world. Grandpa and Grandma were what democracy is all about.

Henry and I spent our free time with the Robies as we tried to put our lives back together. We were beginning to grow desperate for some hope for the future from anywhere, for us and for all the Jewish survivors spread out all over Germany. The Jewish displaced persons, the survivors of concentration camps, were desperately trying to get out of Germany. Having to live among the same people who had persecuted us, who tried to exterminate us, who literally hated all Jews, was extremely difficult. Most of the DPs were still living in barracks, and were searching for any place, any country that would take them in.

Very few countries were offering any sort of help, however. The European countries didn't want us; nor did South America, nor even the United States. Immigration quotas were so restricted that only a trickle of people were being let in, and even then only after years of torturous bureaucratic process. In order to discourage immigrants, the governments of all the countries of the world set up stumbling blocks of red tape. President Harry S. Truman signed the Displaced Persons Act on September 7, 1946, allowing 200,000 displaced persons to enter the United States. But there was a stipulation: They had to be "healthy individuals." How could anyone be healthy after surviving hell? The screening was long and hard, and it took years before the survivors received passports to America. Some countries required you to obtain affidavits from citizens of the country you were emigrating to, stating that you had a means of supporting yourself and would not be a burden to the state. The process was very rigorous. You had to obtain all sorts of papers within certain time frames, and even if you did everything just as required, you were often faced with delays, lost applications, and having to start the whole process all over again from the beginning.

One day Henry remembered that he had a cousin in Brazil. We wrote to him, and after a short correspondence we learned that the only way we could get papers to emigrate to Brazil was if Henry could get a job. The only way he could get a job in a hospital as a doctor, we were told, was if he changed his papers and registered as a non-Jew. Antisemitism had reached the shores of this country also; many Nazi leaders and criminals had escaped to Brazil after the war. Jews were not welcome in this country either. We certainly wouldn't consider denying our religion after all we had suffered for it, and so Brazil was out.

Many Jews wanted to go to Palestine, our historical homeland, which had not yet become Israel. Palestine was at the time in the hands of the British, and they didn't want to let large numbers of Jews in for fear of alienating their Arab neighbors, from whom they wanted oil. Endless negotiations went on between the British and the Arabs of the region. Proposals for a planned Israeli homeland for Jews dwindled on paper from an original proposal which would have followed the boundaries established in the Bible, including the holy city of Jerusalem, to a mere 490 square miles around Tel Aviv, cut in separated chunks around the region, and excluding Jerusalem, which the Arabs wanted to keep. The prospects of us ever getting an official Jewish homeland looked grim.

Despite the British resistance to Jewish settlement in Palestine, many Jews were going there illegally. They felt we could never be welcome in foreign countries, and we had to have our own Jewish homeland, whether the other nations wanted to allow it or not. Rabbi Lipman was one of a large network of people in Germany and throughout Europe working on this illegal immigration to Palestine; he had left the army and was now working with the Jewish Agency. He spent eight months traveling all over the United States, making speeches to raise money to buy ships for illegal immigrants to travel on to Palestine. Then the Agency brought him and his wife and newborn son, Michael, back to Germany.

During Rabbi Lipman's fourteen months in Heidelberg, he visited us often. He had for a long time been working actively to help the displaced persons, and especially the Jews. Many times, he had risked court-martial by arranging illegal transports of Jews to Palestine. During his final post in the army, he had helped to organize an illegal mail service for Jewish survivors to contact relatives and friends around the world. Neither the military nor UNRRA had made any provisions for such mail service, and it remained the only one available to DPs until well into 1947. Now he was even more deeply and radically involved in efforts to help the survivors. He told us about his house in Heidelberg, and how he and his wife Esther used it to house illegal immigrants in transit, as well as to move arms out of the cellar by night. His need to help the survivors was overpowering; he even confided in me once that he found he was jealous of us survivors, that he felt guilty for not having been a concentration camp victim himself. He dealt with these feelings by pouring his whole heart and soul into relief efforts.

Most of his work now consisted of arranging illegal transports of Jews through Germany towards Palestine. Esther worked with him even though she was pregnant; this actually seemed to increase the confidence of the traveling illegals. He told us that they typically took people from Neu-Ulm on Saturday nights, when there were the fewest number of American border guards, through the Black Forest to Pont-de-Seize, where the army had built a pontoon bridge across the Rhine. They would pass French customs with forged documents, then travel on to Mulhouse, where they transferred people to trains for the trip to Marseilles. It was highly illegal, but very well organized. Rabbi Lipman told us that this was the way he wanted us to follow.

It was risky, but Henry and I were ready to leave Germany at any cost. We called my sisters and said goodbye to everyone, all our friends, not telling them where we were going, and we packed up and left Erlangen. We never made it to Palestine, however; we were caught at the border, and were lucky to escape. Back we went to Erlangen, tired and discouraged; fortunately we had not made any arrangements to give up our house, so we were able to return to it. We decided that we would have to wait for America to open its doors and let refugees in. We could only hope that eventually the U.S. would enlarge the quota of Polish Jews who would be allowed in.

Rabbi Lipman, meanwhile, continued his work. The peak of his experience came in July 1947, when his group moved some five thousand people from Germany to Port-de-Bouc near Marseilles in eight days. They all boarded the *Exodus 1947*, bound for Palestine. Unfortunately, the ship was violently captured by the British (three Jews were killed and a hundred wounded); the passengers were taken back to France on British transport ships, and after they staged a hunger strike in the port, the people were forcibly herded back into camps in the British zone of Germany. Eventually, 1,200 of them escaped and were safely transported to Palestine. But after the failure of the *Exodus*, things got progressively more difficult for the illegal immigrants. There was still no way for any significant number of people to get into the United States, and everything seemed to be at a standstill. Rabbi Lipman decided that he could do more from America, working to try to get the borders opened up, so he and Esther returned to the States in time for the birth of their second son.

Henry and I missed the Lipmans, but I had my work to keep me busy. In my office I processed many emigration papers for people of all different nationalities. The wait for our own emigration was getting more and more frustrating. My work was my life in many ways. There was always so much to do, and most days I jumped out of bed and practically ran to work. But one morning in April 1947, I woke up nauseated, my head heavy; I wasn't myself. This went on for days, and finally I told Henry about it. "You must be pregnant," he said as he left for work.

Pregnant? My God, what was I to do? I was the breadwinner in the family. There was no DP hospital in Erlangen, and so Henry had taken a job at the university clinic. But there were no paying jobs for Jewish doctors in German hospitals, so he had been forced to volunteer to work for free. I had to work; I couldn't be pregnant. I thought we had been careful. I didn't understand anything. How I wished my mother was around. I wished I could talk to her about it. I wished a lot of things. But in the meantime, I wasn't feeling well at all. I had to go see a doctor, and since there was no DP hospital here, that meant I had to see a German doctor. All through the night I had nightmares.

"They are going to kill me; they are going to kill my baby!" I had known fear in my life. I had been scared out of my wits during the Holocaust. But never as much as for this new life that was growing inside of me. When I saw the German nurse standing over me, I wouldn't let her touch me. The doctor was an older man, a professor at the university. Henry knew him; he claimed he had not fought the war against the Jews. I tried to convince myself that he was all right, that I was safe. But in my gut, I knew better. Where I came from, there was no safety, no future for a Jewish baby.

Evidently, the doctor had some doubts about me, and kept me in the hospital for two days. On the third day, I was told to go home and rest. I returned to work immediately, however, because I was badly needed. UNRRA was getting out of Germany, and a new organization, the IRO (International Refugee Organization) was taking over. There was much for me to do during the transition.

I was traveling a lot, all over Bavaria, getting bigger, and soon I could feel my baby growing inside of me. I finally began to believe that I was really having a baby! I listened to the heartbeat. I touched my belly. I prayed day and night and dreamed about the baby. My whole life centered around giving life, a new life, a new baby. For all the babies I had seen being killed, I'd give the world a new baby!

The summer passed, and when the autumn leaves were falling I sat at the window and told my unborn child about the fall and about that distant time back in Poland before the war. The times I remembered best were the holidays—Rosh Hashana and Yom Kippur. It was always the beginning of fall. The leaves were changing and the mountains were aflame. We all went to Grandmother's and all us young ones climbed the mountains. We would start early in the morning and watch the sunrise from the mountain top. Then we would rush down the mountain, for there was so much to do on Grandmother's farm. Some of us would milk the cows. Others would feed the chickens. All of us would chase the animals around and around. In the late afternoon we would go up the mountain again. We would climb higher and higher until no one could see us. We would pick berries or just slide on our behinds. We bathed in the sun, hid in the shade. We sang, laughed, and enjoyed our youthfulness. When the vacation was over, we would all return to the city, and to school, and to the winter, which we knew would come soon.

But now I missed my sisters, and arranged for Anna to take the bus to come visit me. We sat and talked and reminisced, although she could hardly remember anything that happened before the war. She mourned Mother and Father and Moshe terribly. A day didn't pass that she didn't bring up their loss. The years of war had made a terrible mark on her. She had a physical mark that served as a constant reminder, too: a bullet wound in her leg that she had received one day back in the ghetto when an SS man had shot her.

Anna believed that it was her destiny to survive, since this bullet could have easily ended her life.

Anna was feeling bitter. "I was so sure the world would embrace us, coming out of hell," she said, "but it didn't happen. We've registered for Canada, America, Australia, and Palestine, and nobody wants us. What are we going to do?" She told me that she and Mania had a plan. There were rumors that the American Joint Distribution Committee in Stuttgart was registering young men and women to make *aliyah* (to go up, as we said in Hebrew) to Palestine. There was a long waiting list, but through my connections, I was able to get them on it, and so the two of them moved to Stuttgart in November 1947. That very month, an important step was taken towards the creation of an independent Jewish homeland when the UN approved the partition of Palestine into Jewish and Arab states. But there was still a ways to go until Israel would finally become an independent state.

In the meantime, winter had arrived, and each day brought me closer to giving birth. I was only working a few hours a day, and when I returned home I rested and waited, and waited. Because Henry was not earning any money, I knew I would have to return to work after the baby was born, so I set about looking for a nurse to take care of my little one. I interviewed many women, and finally found a young German nurse who was very eager to work for me. I had a difficult time with this at first, but I convinced myself that the war was over, and that there were some people who were human beings even though they had been born German.

On the night of December 30, 1947, I was rushed to the hospital to deliver the baby. Henry was on duty that night, but he called for my obstetrician. At 5:15 A.M. my little girl was born. She had blond hair and blue eyes, and she weighed three and a half kilos (seven pounds). We decided to call her Ellen. When I opened my eyes and saw this small bundle next to me, I couldn't believe it. I couldn't yet comprehend that this was my baby, that she was mine and Henry's and she was alive and healthy, and I had given birth to this wonderful new life.

"Dear God," I prayed, "For all the children I have seen murdered, for all the angels we Jews have lost during the war, grant that this child lives and is well and happy, and that she grows up to be a wonderful, happy human being."

But my prayers were not to be answered.

14. Journey into Freedom

On May 14, 1948, Israel finally became a state. This energized a lot of us survivors: finally, there was a place for us. Now there was hope of getting out of Germany. Mania and Anna were still living in Stuttgart, waiting for their papers to go to our newly official Jewish homeland. In the midst of all these dramatic events, Mania was having an exciting new experience of her own. She wrote to me:

"On the day the world celebrated Israel's independence, we all rushed to the city park to rejoice with other Jews. Next to me stood a young man, who started to talk to me. He was about my age, and something about him gave me security. He asked me for a date, and I agreed. I felt good having someone to be with me and protect me. He is a strong man; he is also a survivor, and he speaks the same language I do. I don't mean that he also speaks Polish, which he does, but he knows where I came from and what I've lived through. He understands me; he feels what I feel, and we don't even need words to communicate with each other. I think I'm in love."

I was so happy for my sister. In February 1949 I organized a beautiful wedding for her and Sam in Stuttgart. Unfortunately, the *aliyah* (emigration) to Israel that they and Anna had been waiting for never materialized, and so they turned their energies towards trying once again to get papers for America. Pola and Dolek were also trying to get to the U.S. At the end of March, Pola had given birth to twin boys, and she and Dolek wanted very much not to raise their children in Germany. Anna, meanwhile, met a wonderful young man named Mark, while walking in the streets of

110

Stuttgart one day. He had been hidden by a Christian family all through the war, and had come to Germany looking for surviving members of his family. I felt like a successful maminka: my three sisters all had wonderful men at their sides, and Lola and Stella and Gienia were married, too. Jack and Gienia had a little boy, and Pola and I had beautiful babies. But still, we were all stuck in Germany.

By the spring of 1949 most of the displaced persons had left German DP camps and were reunited with their families. Not so the Jewish people. Six million Jews had been exterminated; one million had survived the atrocities and nobody cared. No one came to help even now. The single fact that the world had allowed this to happen, had looked on and done nothing, kept us awake at night. We knew that no one had moved to help us, even as little children were denying Hitler his victory. My eleven-year-old brother hid day after day without any food or water; he held on heroically until the day he was taken away to a "children's camp," to be pushed into the gas chambers of Auschwitz along with 360 other little children from ages four to fourteen. These innocent children couldn't fight anymore.

I'll never forget the unbelievable courage of my ten-year-old cousin Roman, who hid in the lavatory while the other kids were taken to Auschwitz. He stayed there through days and nights without a crumb, and after all the camp inhabitants had been exterminated, he escaped and spent many months hiding in the woods, all by himself, like a little animal hiding from "civilization," searching for a bite of food, sleeping under the stars, until the end of the war. He survived. My sister Anna survived, too. She was only thirteen years old, and had always to pretend she was older, keeping her back straight and walking tall, for there was no room for Jewish children in Hitler's plan. More than a million children were killed and nobody was moved. Not a soul was moved, and our battle for survival continued. It is impossible to describe how each of us fought to survive.

And where were we now, years after the end of the war? In the midst of Germany, in dilapidated army barracks, on restricted rations, without homes, without families. And the Nazis, the same Germans who killed millions of people, were living free. They were free to move about as they pleased; they had homes; they were with their families. They were respected citizens of their country, while we Jews had no place to go.

We all struggled for years with the arduous emigration process. Sometimes it seemed we would never get to America, never get out of Germany. But finally, the years of waiting came to an end. Sam and Mania, seven months pregnant at the time, left for America in September 1949. Pola and Dolek, with their twin boys, followed on October 6th; because they had little babies they were given the opportunity to fly instead of going by boat. Finally, Anna left that same month. Mark's papers had not come through yet, and so they had to be separated. This broke Anna's heart, but she could wait no longer to get out of Germany. My sisters had all made it to the *goldeneh medina*, the golden land, America. Gienia and Jack were to make the trip themselves in December. Would it ever be my turn?

One day I called Henry at work. He could tell by my voice that something was going on, but before he could get a word out, I blurted: "Our papers arrived! We can go to America!" He was speechless. I had filled out the applications so long ago, and our waiting had gone on so long, that he had given up. And now, here it was: we could leave Germany! We could finally leave everything behind. Perhaps he could even leave his nightmares behind. I knew that he suffered terribly. I could hear his screams many a night, but he refused to talk about it. He had been one of the first to be taken to Auschwitz, and had stayed there three years. How did he ever survive it? What hell he lived through I would never know, for he never was able to talk about it. He lived alone with his pain and the memories of hell all his life.

On October 1, 1949, Henry and I, together with our beloved Ellen, were called to the emigration office and were told to report to the German consul's office in Hamburg. I prayed especially hard this day. I knew that I should be happy; my dreams were coming true. We were going to America! We were going to start a new life! We were finally going to be free! But somehow, it was all so hard. There was so much to do, so much to think about: getting through all the formalities of emigration; leaving behind some—albeit very little—security, a job, and a home; going to a strange country; not knowing anybody there. I was so confused and scared; but I knew that no matter what it took, it was time to leave Germany—and our nightmares—behind.

We arrived in Hamburg and were placed in a camp. The next day we were to report for the medical examinations. We stood in lines forever. We were so frightened; there were strange faces all around us and no one to talk to. Henry was called into the doctor's office, and Ellen and I went with him. The doctor was very impersonal, and I felt like saying, "My husband is a doctor, too; can't you treat him with some respect?" Instead, I just sat there and waited.

When the X-rays were taken and the examination was completed, the doctor simply said: "Sorry, Dr. Rubinstein, you aren't eligible. You can't go to America. Your X-ray shows that there is something wrong with your lungs. The emigration authorities won't let you through." End of story. We were unable to move. We couldn't believe what we had just heard. It couldn't be. "Oh, God," I prayed, "don't let this be true." The doctor just looked at us. He showed no understanding of what his words were doing to us. He couldn't begin to imagine.

When we finally left the office I put my arms around Henry and cried. Ellen cried, too. I held her close to my heart, and her warmth gave me some strength and hope. Hand in hand, Henry and I walked back to the barracks.

The sight of the barracks brought me to my senses. Never again will I stay in a barrack, I swore. Never again will I feel like a prisoner! I am not a prisoner anymore. I will never be a prisoner again! I collected all my energy and swept up our meager belongings. Deliberately we left the camp, and with the little money we had, we checked into an inn for the night.

We had a nice clean bed, and a small bed for Ellen, but I never closed my eyes.

"We can't go to America," I repeated over and over in my head. What did it mean? How could we live in Germany permanently? It was difficult enough to live here temporarily, but to stay forever and ever . . . to stay in Germany for the rest of our lives? How could we really live among the Germans? We had been in their country for four and a half years, and we were still afraid to walk the streets. We would always imagine that they could kill us; we were and always would be afraid of the Germans. "God," I prayed, "help me to forget; if not to forgive, then at least to forget. I can't live with this fear for the rest of my life." But what if we had no other options?

The wind was blowing and the snowflakes were falling as I walked out of the inn in the morning. I found out where the IRO office was: surely the International Refugee Organization, the successor to UNRRA, could help me. After all, I had been working for UNRRA for five years. I had helped thousands of people to emigrate. When I got to the IRO office, I insisted on seeing the director; I showed him the letter of recommendation given to me by the IRO in Erlangen. He promised to do what he could. When I left his office, I went straight to the director of the American Joint Distribution Committee, a Jewish agency that was in Germany to help the Jewish emigrants.

Two days later Henry had another X-ray taken. There was a conference between the German doctor and the emigration officials. We waited on pins and needles for the decision. The next day we received a pass to report to the transportation chairman. After all we had been through, I was oblivious to my feelings. I acted like a robot, following instructions and moving automatically from one office to another. I was unable to believe that we were ever going to get out of Germany. But it turned out that Henry's problem wasn't too serious, probably some damage from malnutrition. And, somehow, the intervention from the IRO representative had helped. We received our clearance.

114

On December 1, 1949, we began our journey into freedom. We boarded the Navy ship *General Taylor* to sail to the United States of America. Henry reported to the ship's captain and told him that he was a doctor. He was immediately engaged as a medical doctor for the journey. Ellen and I took a bunk bed in a small cabin; Henry was given a cabin with the crew. We had a little round window through which we could see the world. As soon as the ship started moving, Ellen and I got seasick. Henry tried his best to revive us; he brought us medicine and food, but nothing helped. It was that difficult time of the year when the ocean roars and the waves reach for the skies; the ship was being tossed up and down like a balloon. Most of the people on board were very sick; after all our waiting, we didn't care whether we reached the shores of America dead or alive.

But when the ship finally glided into New York harbor, Henry rushed to find us, took Ellen in his arms, and pulled me out on deck to see the Statue of Liberty. I can still close my eyes and see it standing there through the fog. All I could think was: This is the Statue of Liberty. Liberty means freedom. We are offered freedom, freedom to live, to speak, to enjoy. Freedom from fear. Freedom . . . My heart was heavy, my body was ill, and my mind was clouded, but I felt such joy!

I went back into the cabin, sat on my bed, and embraced my darling daughter. I rocked her, even though the boat had stopped rocking. I told her that we had arrived. I told her that we had come here to start a new life. I told her that Daddy and I had a dream, and that this dream was coming to America, and it had come true!

Did Ellen understand what I was talking about? Did she know; did she feel her parents' hope? She was only two years old, and yet, I believe that she did know.

Part Three
Many Roads to Freedom

15. Janka's Story: Through the War in Russia

Even though we were about to start a new life in America, my thoughts were still with all the people I had met after the war. I had helped thousands of people to find a place to live, to emigrate, to start new lives, just as I was about to do. Their stories swam in my head. I remembered one woman who had walked into my office with frustration boiling over in her eyes. She started talking so fast I could hardly follow her.

"I have a little baby, my husband and I must go to the United States, you must help me. We were not here, not in concentration camps; we were in Russia, in the North Pole, terrible, terrible," she cried.

I really wanted to hear her story, for I hadn't met many people who had spent the war in Russia. But I had such a great load on my desk, I knew I couldn't give her enough time, and so I asked her if she could come back about four P.M., and I would spend the time with her only. Janka was her name, and this is the story she related to me.

*   *   *

I lived in the eastern part of Poland, and after the Russians occupied the area, they shipped thousands of us into the North Pole. I had been imprisoned, not for any crime I had committed, but only because I was from Poland; the Russians took all the young, able-bodied people they could round up to work for them in deep into Russia. We didn't know much about what happened in Poland during the war, and we only hoped that one day it would be over, and that we'd be able to return home.

I was working in the kitchen, and a Russian cook was teaching me how to prepare food for the prisoners, who occupied the whole area around us. I had to take the kettle outside and dish out the food, but my hands were freezing and sometimes my fingers would stick to the ladle. I remember that my hands were covered with blisters, and one day another woman had to take over for me.

This was the end of 1945, and there was talk around the camp that the war was over. One day the commandant walked into the kitchen and began reading names from a list of prisoners who were to be freed. I listened. I heard him call my name. I'm free, I thought, but where will I go? I have no money, no clothes, nothing. Now that I'm no longer a prisoner, I'll starve; they will not feed me. I was in a state of panic. The area where I was imprisoned was isolated from the rest of the world, except for another camp in which thousands of German soldiers were imprisoned. They were treated terribly by the Russians, and many hundreds were dying every day. They were tortured, and their screams echoed all the way to our camp. I had heard that on the other side of the camp was a camp for men from Poland. A Russian woman that I had befriended kept insisting that I go to the men's camp, where she would introduce me to a man who would help me get away from the North Pole.

One day she brought me a dress, and we began the long journey to the men's camp together. I was only nineteen years old, and I was very frightened, but my Russian friend insisted: "Don't worry, Janka, I'll make sure that you get there safely. I think you will like this man. Together we'll find help for you."

When we reached the men's camp, the prisoners were working in a coal mine. I was introduced to the overseer; he worked indoors distributing food and clothing. I knew immediately that I had seen him before. I searched my memory trying to recall where I could have met him. Suddenly, I remembered: it was on the boat coming to the North

Pole. He had been so helpful and encouraging. We all thought that we were running away from persecution, escaping the Germans, to be free, to be saved by the Russians. We couldn't have been more wrong. But at least we were alive. I stood in front of the overseer, and he looked at me as a complete stranger. My heart was filled with emotion, for this young boy had grown into an old man in only three years. I wondered whether the years of hard labor, hunger, and cold had left such a mark on me that he couldn't recognize me. Was there anything left of the young girl who had been torn from her parents' home only a few years ago?

All of these thoughts were rushing through me at once. I looked at this man; his face commanded respect, but his eyes held a softness and love. We began to speak in Polish, and the Russian woman who had brought me looked at us in amazement. I felt as though I had found a long lost friend in Stefan. Unfortunately, I soon learned that he would be a prisoner for another year, and I could only visit him once a week for two hours.

I visited Stefan continuously for the next few months, and it didn't take long before we fell in love. One day he asked me to marry him. He wanted to take care of me, and share his food with me, for I was getting very little. Stefan found a Russian official who married us, and we were assigned to a barrack for married couples. The barrack was divided into thirty small rooms. There was one kitchen for all of us. Every night, there were thirty women in this kitchen trying to cook dinner for their families. We had so little. In the midst of all these troubles, I became pregnant. I had such cravings, but the only thing I could indulge myself with was sugar. I would eat it by the spoonful whenever I was hungry.

Another winter was coming. The days were getting shorter, and we knew that the endless night would soon engulf us; we knew that soon we wouldn't be able to move. The thought of having a baby under these conditions frightened us. Finally, in desperation, Stefan decided to appeal for freedom. His case was reconsidered; he was granted a release. He had freedom, but what could we do with it? He couldn't leave the North Pole without a passport, and the only place he could obtain a passport was in Moscow, thousands of miles away.

Stefan decided that he had to take a chance. He now had a family to think about. After taking a boat to the mainland, he went to the railway station. He hid under coal loads, jumping from train to train, and walked when he had to, for thousands of miles. I was so worried about him. Just when I was about to give up hope, he returned. I hardly recognized him. He had lost so much weight, he looked like a skeleton, but he had a smile on his face. I was so proud of his courage, when he told me what he had had to do to get to Moscow and to get the necessary papers. He reached into his bag and pulled out forty passports for fellow prisoners.

I was by now five months pregnant, and we decided to leave immediately. The only transportation we could find was a coal train. The trip was horrendous. We had icicles all over our bodies. After a couple of days without any food, I was too weak even to get off the train. Stefan carried me into the train station; he was hoping we could catch a train to Moscow. He argued with all the officials. "We have to get away from here; my wife is going to have a baby; my visa will expire soon," he yelled. Finally, one Russian official listened to his laments and promised that a train would come from Ural and take us west. We waited. The train came and whisked by the station. Our hearts sank. The official motioned desperately for the train to stop; suddenly, about a mile away from the station, it did. We had to run to catch it, but I still couldn't move my legs. Stefan literally carried me all the way. When we reached the train, Stefan lifted me into a seat. The train was filled with wounded soldiers, young boys without arms or legs returning from the war, sick and devastated.

Spring was in the air when we finally reached Moscow. We were confused, starved, and barely able to move. We found the Polish embassy. We received some food, clothes, and finally visas and tickets to go by train to the eastern part of Poland. We wanted to think that we were finally free, but this was not quite true. When we reached the Polish border, we were interrogated for hours: "Why did you leave Poland? Where have you been all these years? Why are you coming back? Are you spies?" After many hours of questioning, the official finally let us go, and we crossed the border into Poland. Our bodies were tired, our minds confused, and our stomachs empty. I was so worried about the baby. I wanted to make sure that everything was all right. Yes, I dreamed about my mother and father, and yes, I longed to be with them and for them to meet my beloved Stefan; but first and foremost I wanted a bowl of hot soup and a warm bed.

The train came to a halt in Lwow. We stepped off the train and I'm sure that we must have looked quite a sight. There we were, in our Eskimo clothes and big boots looking like we were expecting a blizzard. Here it was, a warm day in May, and we were happy to feel the warmth of the sun. A young man stopped us and asked where we had come from. He was a newspaper reporter. He offered to pay us ten *zloty* (Polish money) for our story. We found a place to talk, and told him about our journey. When we finished, he gave us the money and we were on our way.

Our first stop was the office of the American Joint Distribution Committee. We were desperate for information about our families. It took us a couple of days to contact everyone we knew, and every Jewish person we could locate in town, but by the end of the week, we knew what we had dreaded. We had lost everybody. They were all dead, according to the information we received. All through the years in Russian prison camps, I believed that I was all alone in the world, but during the journey back to Poland I had tried to hold onto the hope that some of my family would be alive. Now all my hopes and dreams were destroyed. My mother and father, my younger sister, all my relatives were gone. I was so glad to have Stefan by my side. We were both orphans, but at least we had each other.

Stefan and I knew that the war was over; we knew that we were free, but we also knew that there was no home for us to go to. Stefan didn't want to discuss the fact that we were homeless. "Freedom has a price," he would say. "We won't talk about freedom," he insisted. "We won't talk about our parents, our brothers and sisters. We won't talk about the war and the atrocities. We'll just look towards our future," he reasoned. What future? Where could we go? We each had many questions and no answers.

*　　　*　　　*

Janka broke down and cried, and I tried to cheer her up. Carefully, I said: "Stefan is right. You survived and you can now look into the future. Let's see what we can do." They had been assigned a small apartment in Lwow, where they had lived for six months after reaching Poland. But there were always Russian soldiers around, and wherever they went they felt hostility all around them. They had managed to get to Germany through illegal channels, and now they needed my help. Janka wanted me to help find a place for her and Stefan and their baby daughter to stay, and hopefully to help them emigrate to the United States. I advised Janka to come in the morning with Stefan and the baby, and I would see what I could do for them.

Janka and Stefan's struggle for freedom was not soon over. They had to live in DP camps, in very difficult conditions, for another two years. During this time they had a son, and because they had two small children, they were able to get to America sooner than some of the other Jewish survivors in the camps. In February 1950, they finally made it. They had thought they would find the streets paved with gold, but they still had to struggle just to get from one day to the next. Their American neighbors did not greet them with open arms, but stayed as far away as they could, and the years of slavery in Russian prison camps were not the distant memory Janka and Stefan hoped they would be. After many years of perseverance and hard work, however, they found their own road to recovery. And, with their children and grandchildren, they could finally enjoy their freedom.

16. Lena's Story: Life in a Bunker

Janka's journey from persecution into freedom was long and hard, but so, unfortunately, were the journeys of thousands of other mothers and their children. I remembered another unbelievable story that a mother brought to me. I was working on emigration papers when a woman walked into my office with a small boy holding tightly to her skirt. His eyes were wide open and his mouth tightly closed. He looked like a frightened animal when his mother spoke to me. I found living quarters for them while they were waiting for emigration papers to the United States. During their wait, a very special relationship developed between us.

Many times Lena tried to tell me her story, but somehow we could never find enough time, until one day she brought me a letter that she had written to her son, for him to read when he grew up.

*   *   *

My son,

It all seems like ages ago, but it wasn't really. I'm talking about the time you were born, my son, the first boy in the family, our first child. How proud your father was! I can still see him giving out cigars. Everybody had to know that he had a son. You were born very small, about five pounds. When I look at you now, I can hardly believe it. I remember the songs I sang for you and how you giggled as if you too wanted to sing. Soon your laughter became our happiness and your cry was our cry. Our lives were built around you. Preoccupied with you and your comforts, I was hardly aware of what was happening in the world around us. It wasn't long, however, before the shadows of war reached our peaceful home.

News about the persecution of the Jews was coming from all over. People were running, disappearing, but where and how nobody would tell. Before I realized it, half the city was gone. Raids were organized at night and young as well as old were taken out of their beds, out of their homes, and shipped away. Families were torn apart, and terrible news of mass murder, shootings, gassings spread across the countryside.

What should we do? Where could we run with a little creature like you? It was all so confusing. We couldn't understand why we should run. We never hurt anybody. We didn't fight this war; why would anyone want to hurt us, hurt our little baby? We asked ourselves these questions, but we had no answers. All we knew was that the Germans were killing the Jews, and we had to do something if we wanted to survive.

One day your father came up with a plan. He would build a shelter, a room for you and me. The room would be built under the house of a Gentile friend who lived outside the Jewish section of town. He was a good friend of your father's, and he would be the only one who would know that we were there. Millions of difficult questions came to my mind: What about food? How could you grow without fresh air? What about long walks through the park to strengthen your lungs? How could you grow up in a little prison cell, without light or water?

In a couple of days, our shelter under the house was built, and you and I moved into our new "home." Your father had to stay on the outside so he could bring us food and water during the night, hoping that no one would see him. We took very few belongings with us. After all, how long would we, could we, stay in the bunker? The war would be over soon, and we'd be free again. How little we knew. Would you believe it, you were crying all the way to the shelter. I almost thought that you understood what was happening.

It was a long way from home. We had to be careful not to be noticed by anyone, and I had to cover your mouth so your crying wouldn't be heard. In a way we were fleeing from the world and from the war. I was taking you away from it all to save you, to hide you. As we entered our tiny room I shivered, for this was the smallest prison cell I had ever imagined, a room without a window. The door was built into the wall so no one could see it. Only the owner of the house knew we were there, and only your father would enter. At no time would we be able to leave this room. How can one live through such a sentence? How long will we have to endure, I wondered, and with that thought, a great fear entered my soul.

The first days went by. I held you in my arms, and sang quietly so no one would hear me. Days went into nights, and when you slept I was happy for I didn't have to keep you quiet. My nights were full of dreams. Maybe this night will be the last. Maybe tomorrow your father will come and tell us that the war is over and that we can come out and see the world.

Early one morning your father brought us food and told me that he wouldn't be able to come anymore. He had to leave town. He had given some money to the man above us, who would bring us food from now on. I kissed your father tenderly, and a part of me died forever.

All through this day I held you tightly in my arms and whispered: "Don't worry, my love, I'll save you." I told you stories and made plans for your future. Once you were going to be a musician. You were going to make music like nobody ever did before. Another time you were going to build bridges, longer and higher than anyone had ever built. But on the days when you were sick and I couldn't call a doctor, I imagined that you were a doctor and that you could heal yourself. I followed your instructions: "Hold me in your arms, Mother," you seemed to beg. I cuddled you and kept you warm, close to my heart. The Lord has always been with us because your illnesses ended.

Not so the war, however. At first I marked the days on the calendar, then weeks and then months. The year passed and the calendar was finished. I stopped counting. I walked across the little room and talked to you, but you didn't say a word. I was so scared; I thought you would never be able to speak. You were growing slowly, but the food rations were getting smaller; on many days the man from upstairs didn't show up, and we went hungry all day. You were already four years old and not a sound did you make. Some days I believed you wanted to say something, but only an inaudible whisper came out. Most of the time I was pleased that you couldn't talk for fear someone might hear us.

It was the spring of 1945. Our messenger came in one day and told me that the war was at an end. "The Russians are coming," he said. Soon after that, we heard a tremendous detonation and an explosion outside. Our house was trembling. I lay next to you and told you stories about the time when there was no war, no bombs, and no fear for the young to grow old, and you looked at me in bewilderment. It must have all seemed very odd to you; after all, the only world you knew was the one in which we lived. In all the confusion you went to sleep. I sat by your side. The terrible stillness of the night frightened me. There was no one I could ask what had happened and no one I could turn to for help. I imagined that the explosion had taken the lives of all the people in town and only the two of us had survived.

I got dressed; I had to have a look outside. I had not been outside for three years. I was truly afraid to step out; I was afraid of what I would find. I pushed the door open and walked up into the courtyard. I took a deep breath, unaccustomed as I was to the fresh air, and I realized that my strength was failing. I had difficulty walking, but I took a few steps and all was quiet. The houses nearby were down and people buried under them. There were dead bodies all around me. I stumbled and fell; I couldn't move. I don't know how long I was there, but suddenly, I thought I heard a whimper, a cry. I hurried back to our shelter as fast as my feet would carry me. I took you into my arms and tears were rolling down my cheeks as you repeated: "Mama, Mama, Mama." Those were the most wonderful words I ever heard. You could speak! I was so happy.

I found some clothes that I had made for you and dressed you the best I could, and hand in hand we walked out of our prison. We reached some streets that were familiar to me, and yet they looked strange. The houses were bombed, streets were covered with rubbish, and there was no sign of people. We reached a different part of town, and here men and women were running in different directions, yelling, screaming, looking for others. I learned from them that the war was over. The war was over, but people were still dying; the Germans were making one last strike to kill everybody they could.

I found the house where we had lived before, but it was demolished, and all my efforts to locate someone from our family were in vain. Little by little I learned that there were no Jews left in Poland. The Germans had exterminated them and the Poles didn't even want the ones who had miraculously survived. I was advised to leave as soon as I could, but where I should go and how, nobody knew. First of all I had to find a place where we could live and sleep. We had to have a roof over our heads. A very gracious Polish woman took us in. Your movements were very restricted in the beginning, but slowly you began to walk, and I made you jump and run. Time passed before you began to talk—very slowly at first, but I worked with you every day and you started talking to me, quietly but clearly. You soon found children to play with and in no time acted like a normal five-year-old boy.

Five years of worries, fears, and starvation started to take effect on me. I was scared to death. I worried that I would not be able to take care of you, so I desperately began to search for your father. We moved from place to place, from city to city, looking for familiar faces and gathering what information we could. We learned that a number of people who had survived lived in Germany in displaced persons camps under the care of UNRRA, the United Nations. We moved on. One day we learned that your father had survived and lived in the camp in Struth, Germany. I don't have to tell you about this reunion, because I know that you remember it so well. This was one of the greatest days the three of us lived to share. Once we were together again, we decided to register for emigration to the United States. We hope that because children are a priority we won't have to wait too long.

Even though our struggle isn't yet over, we are free; you are free, my son. The fears, the hatred must be forgotten. You can now breathe the fresh air; you will learn that people of all kinds can live together and work together. Yes, my son, you are free at last.

*   *   *

I read this letter again and again, and I can still remember so clearly the day Lena and her little boy walked into my office.

I will never forget the wonderful day when I was able to hand them their papers to leave for America.

Lena's little boy did indeed grow up to become a physician, just as Lena had imagined, and on the day of his graduation from medical school, she gave him the letter she had written all those years ago.

17. Miroslawa's Story: Righteous Gentiles

Even after I arrived in the United States, I continued to meet people who had survived the war. It surprised me, here in this new country, to meet up with other survivors. But somehow we always seemed to find each other. Sometimes the people I met up with were old acquaintances, or even family members. I found a cousin of mine, Fred, in this way. Fred had been in Plaszow with us. One day while he was working in the camp with his father and his eleven-year-old brother, the commandant had come in and, for no particular reason, shot Fred's father and brother, right in front of him. Fred was just thirteen years old at the time. He had miraculously survived, and made it to America, where he went to high school and then college, and became very successful in business.

Fred married a lovely woman named Miroslawa, also a survivor from Poland. At their wedding celebration, I had a chance to meet her and to hear her incredible story. Miroslawa was born Jewish in 1942, in the midst of the war. Her story is unique. Most of it was told to her by her Polish mother who adopted her.

* * *

Some Jewish families had already been taken into the ghetto, and rumor had it that all Jewish children would be killed. My father asked his Polish neighbor if he could take me and keep me through the war. This Polish couple had two grown children, and they promised my father that they would think about it. By the time they decided, our whole family had been taken to the ghetto. This Polish couple risked their lives by walking into the ghetto, pretending to be Jewish. They wore yellow stars on their arms as the Jews had to, and they walked out of the ghetto holding a laundry basket, with a little bundle fast asleep under the linens. My parents tried desperately to find someone who would take my five-year-old brother out of the ghetto, too, but nobody would shelter him because he was circumcised, and anyone could see that he was Jewish.

My Polish foster mother later told me that she had imagined that she would take me home for a few days, and the war would be over, and my parents would get out of the ghetto and come for me. I was there for about three months when my real mother sneaked out of the ghetto, risking her life—for by that point no one was allowed out anymore—and came to say good-bye to me, for she knew that they were being shipped away soon. She had no idea where they were going. She promised the Polish woman that she would come back for me as soon as the war was over.

The Polish couple never told anyone they were sheltering a Jewish child. But one day, six months before the end of the war, the caretaker of our apartment called the SS and told them that this Polish couple was hiding a Jewish child. When the Germans came into our house, my mother told them boldly that I was her daughter's illegitimate child. In the meantime she had sent her nineteen-year-old daughter away for fear that she might tell them the truth.

My Polish mother was a real fighter. She insisted that she was telling them the truth, and she sounded very convincing. In spite of her efforts the Germans took her, her husband, and me to prison. I was only three years old, but I vividly remember the cell. I was very frightened, and the other women were talking to me and showing me all kinds of games. My father was in a cell next to us, and my mother was trying to communicate with him. She would repeat the stories that she had told the Germans so that he would tell the same stories, for they were interrogated constantly.

We were imprisoned for a month, and after our release

the Germans continued to come to the house and ask more questions. My mother was very insistent. She would say: "What do you want me to do? Do you want me to give away my granddaughter, the child of my child?" Strangely enough, I was very dark, my hair was black, and the only thing I could have had of her daughter's were my eyes. They were blue like the sky.

The SS men tried to talk to me in German, thinking that if I had ever heard some Yiddish, the language Jews spoke, then I would understand German, for Yiddish and German are very close to each other. But I just looked at them; I certainly didn't know what they were talking about. I had been just a baby when my parents left me with my Polish foster parents. I had never known any language but Polish. When the SS men spoke their incomprehensible language to me, sometimes I would reach for their guns and play with them.

One day the Germans came and took my father away. I waited for him day after day. I stood at the window and watched for him to come back, but he never came. A few days before the end of the war my mother received a little piece of paper someone had smuggled out of the concentration camp Matthausen, which was somewhere in Austria, telling her that her husband was killed. My mother and I were left alone. My father was the only real breadwinner in the family. My mother's real daughter came back to live with us, for she too had no money and no support. We were all very, very poor. We lived in utter poverty. Many nights I went to sleep hurting from hunger.

In the beginning of May 1945, we learned that the war was over. But for us nothing changed. My mother was working very hard, taking in any sort of piecemeal job she could get. For a while she was making gloves for people who worked in the dye factory. She never left me alone, but kept me sitting by her side as she cut and sewed the gloves. She would tell me stories and read books to me.

Sometime during 1946, two young men walked into our house and claimed to be my cousins: my mother's sister's sons. They told my mother that their aunt, my real mother, had given someone a note before she was exterminated at Auschwitz. The scrap of paper had my Polish mother's address on it, and they were glad to find me. They wanted to take me with them, but she told them quite clearly that the only people she would give me back to would be to my own parents. She did, however, mention to them that if they cared to come back in a few years it might be different, because after all she wasn't getting any younger. They never showed up.

In the autumn of 1947, the situation at home was critical. There was hardly any food to sustain us. Being only five years old, I wasn't aware of any catastrophe, but as my Polish mother related to me much later, she was afraid that I would die from starvation.

One day a woman who lived in the neighborhood and was aware of our situation suggested that my mother find some work in town and put me in a foster home, which this woman supervised. I could stay in the foster home during the week, and on weekends my mother could take me home. My mother knew that this woman was one of the few Jews who had come back after the war, and she was grateful for this idea. She packed some clothes for me, and we walked to the foster home.

At first I was excited to be among children, but I missed my mother terribly. Before I went to sleep, I knelt and prayed, but I noticed the other children didn't. I said my prayers quietly before every meal, for the food was good even though it was different from what my mother had at home. On Friday night the woman lit candles and everybody stood around her. The dinner on Friday night was very festive. The man of the house had a beard and covered his head with something, and the woman wore a scarf on her head. She even covered her eyes when she was praying. I found it all very strange, and I missed my home and my mother more and more. I cried myself to sleep every night.

My mother also missed me terribly, and one day she appeared and told the woman that she would like to take me home. The woman begged her to leave me for one more week. She explained that she understood why I was unhappy. She said that the other children were also confused because of me. The children were all Jewish, and they couldn't understand my ways, my kneeling, praying; they had different customs and traditions. But she was willing to convince these children that I could have my way and they could have theirs.

My mother seemed appeased, and after much urging she left me for one more week. The next Friday when she came for me, I was gone. Where was I? What had they done to me? My Polish mother lamented and cried, but she got no answer. I was gone.

This was March 1948. I remember it so well. I was already getting used to the foster home. I didn't love it, but I had enough food, and I could play with the other children all day; I wasn't crying so much any more. One morning an old man I had never seen before came to the foster home, took my belongings, and told me I was going to take a trip. I was so frightened of this man, a complete stranger, and frightened that I'd never see my mother again. I was crying and jumping around; I didn't want to go. The man gave me candy, held my hand, and walked me to the train station. I was so scared, I couldn't even talk. We got on the train, and as soon as it moved, I fell asleep. I held a little doll that my mother had given me when she last visited me, and I imagined that I was going home.

The jerk of the train awakened me, and I was pulled off the train by the old man. We spent many hours at the station going through security. I fell asleep on the floor. When I opened my eyes, I saw a man standing over me, and I thought I was dreaming. I thought this man was a monster who had come to take me away. The man had a sort of sheet over his head and funny things over his arms. The security man came over to me and tried to explain things to me, telling me that this man was just praying for me and that he wore a prayer shawl. He didn't mean to hurt me. He was surprised that I didn't know this man and asked me what I was doing here and who brought me in.

I turned around; I couldn't answer his questions. I only wanted to go home; I wanted my mommy. The security man went into the other room and found the old man who had brought me into the station. He checked his papers and learned that the man had a false passport for me. He started to ask him questions, but the man was so infuriated with the security check that he told the security man he didn't know anything about me at all.

The security man took me into his room, handed me some food, and told me to wait for him. When he finished work for the day, he took me to his home, and he and his wife took care of me for the next two months. They were so nice to me; they even shared their bed with me. I felt warm and safe, and I wasn't hungry. They had no children and treated me as if I was their own child, but during the night I would wake up and cry for my mother. I missed her terribly. Some days I wouldn't stop crying at all. This couple understood my pain, and decided to find my mother. I didn't know the address, but I knew that we lived in Sosnowiec. I knew that there was a bake shop on one side of our little house and another shop on the other side. I also told the man that my mother worked and brought home food. The security man went to Sosnowiec, and after a few days he found my mother and brought her to me.

My mother walked into the house and I ran to her. We knelt on the floor and hugged and kissed and cried for hours. We were so happy to be together again. My mother found out from the security officer that the old man who had kidnapped me was planning to take me to Palestine. Palestine at the time was still in the hands of the British, who had very stringent immigration quotas. But there was an organization concerned with Jewish children, of whom so few survived the war, that was trying to get them to Palestine through an illegal immigration network. There the children would be given to Jewish parents to be raised as Jews. The old man would have succeeded in taking me to Palestine if it hadn't been for the security man, who recognized the passport the man held for me as false. My mother was so grateful to the security man and his wife for all they had done for me, that the three of them remained friends forever.

I was so happy to be with my mother again. I knew very little about the war, but although it had ended years before, the aftermath was still being felt all over Europe. I did not know that she was not my real mother; I did not know that I was born Jewish. I did not realize that my Jewish heritage would make people hunt me. Jews from all over the world believed that each and every Jewish child who had managed to survive the horrors of the Holocaust had to be raised Jewish, to continue the Jewish people and save them from assimilation. Once they learned that I had been left by a Jewish mother, they wanted to reunite me with my Jewish family. And so the hunt had begun.

One day my mother was called to court. I was so scared, I held onto her skirt all through the proceedings. This happened several times, until one day the judge, tired of all these court motions, made a decision. He didn't want to hear this case anymore until I turned eighteen years old. Then I would decide for myself who and what I wanted to be. My mother took me to church and had me baptized and went with me to communion. Somehow, I remember this whole day as a transformation, some kind of clearing up of body and soul. Everything else that had happened before escaped my memory, and it was like I was just born at baptism. I was a seven-year-old Catholic girl, born to my mother, the only mother I knew and loved. I went to church every Sunday. I attended school regularly, and I was a very good student. I was a happy child.

When I was about thirteen years old some children in my class called me "Jewess, Jewess, dirty Jewess." I came home and asked my mother why they would call me that. What did it mean? My mother took me into her arms and explained to me that there are people who do not believe in Jesus Christ. She told me that oftentimes these non-Christians have dark skin like me, and that maybe this was the reason the kids called me that. She assured me that I was a good Catholic, and I mustn't pay any attention to them.

Years later when I was sixteen, I was on a date with my boyfriend, and some kids walking by again called "Jewess, Jewess." I was so angry and embarrassed that I left my boyfriend and ran home. I told my mother that something must be wrong with me, and she'd better tell me. The look on her face frightened me. She was as white as a sheet; she slumped down on a chair. She let out a sigh, took a deep breath, and told me the whole story.

My mother cried and cried. She told me how she carried me out of the ghetto to save me. She told me that her husband was killed because he had sheltered a Jewish child. She assured me that she loved me with all her heart, because otherwise it would have been impossible for her to live through all these difficult times with me and the constant fear of being discovered. I cried with my mother, and I believe that I cried because I loved her, but I also cried for myself. I didn't know who I was. This wasn't my real mother, so who was? I wasn't a Catholic, so who was I? What did it mean to be Jewish? I was filled with questions, questions, and more questions.

I urged my Polish mother to tell me all about my real parents. She told me that my mother was a shy woman, that she was beautiful. She mentioned that my mother had given her some jewelry for me, but her husband hid it somewhere and she couldn't find it. My father gave her two hundred zloty, which she used to feed us when we were starving to death. She wanted me to know that the greatest tragedy my real parents lived through was having to give me away. They really loved me and wanted to save my life, no matter what. She recalled the day my mother left me for the last time. She said good-bye, and walked slowly away from the house. As she walked, she stopped and picked a leaf off a maple tree and threw it high into the air, as if she'd just shed a leaf off of her own tree.

Several years later I learned from some witnesses that my mother was killed in the gas chambers of Auschwitz, and my brother died there too. My father was shot in another concentration camp. I was never able to get a picture of my mother, and I'll forever have to imagine what she looked like. Her picture changes in my heart as I grow older.

I was dazed by what I had learned. Who am I? What's happening to me? How am I to proceed with my life? Where should I turn for help? My dreams haunted me, and I would awaken in the middle of the night screaming and crying.

On my eighteenth birthday, I awoke to a bright and sunny day. I turned on the radio and heard a voice from far, far away. The voice sounded loud and clear, even though it came from America. "The Jewish Agency in New York is sending people to Poland to search for Jewish children who may have survived the war. They will be reunited with their families, whenever possible." I didn't mention it to my mother because she was already scared. She knew that I had started investigating my Jewish heritage. She loved me so, and she was afraid to lose me.

One day I came home after school and found two strangers sitting in the room talking to my mother. I soon learned that they had come all the way from America. One of the men, a Mr. Gross, was a very orthodox Jew who lived by the words of the Torah. At home he had a beard and *peyos*, sidecurls, for the Torah says that a man must not shave his beard. But he had shaved off his beard and cut off his *peyos* before coming to Poland, in order not to be immediately recognizable as a Jew, for he had heard that the Polish people were very antisemitic. He was searching for Jewish children, and he believed that all his sins would be forgiven by God if he saved a Jewish child. Over one million Jewish children had been killed by Hitler, and to save a Jewish child was a good deed indeed, for if the few Jewish children still alive were not raised as Jews, they would be lost to the Jewish people as surely as if they had been killed. So, these men would take these children to America and educate them to be good Jews. Mr. Gross believed that this was his mission in life.

At first he tried to bribe me. He told me that in America everything was bigger and better than in Poland. He told me that in America I'd have more and better food, beautiful clothes, good schools, and many friends.

My mind was boggled; I was utterly confused. I listened to him, yet deep in my heart I knew I loved my Polish mother. I didn't think I could leave her. She loved me, I knew that. After her husband was killed, she would say to me, "You know, my darling, we are both orphans now." But I would cheer her up: "No, Mother, I do not feel like an orphan. I have you, and I have a home; I don't feel deprived at all." I really didn't feel deprived, but I was confused. This man was telling me about all the things I could have never even dared to dream. I listened to him, and he inspired me more and more. He told me that he could get me into the best school in New York, Stern College; there would be no problem getting me in.

My mother was worried sick. To her this was a young man who wanted to take away her beautiful child and perhaps sell her as a prostitute. She couldn't comprehend why these total strangers would want to help me. In a terrible rage and with many harsh words, she ordered them to leave her home and never come back.

Six weeks later one of the men appeared again, but this time he came with his wife, Mrs. Gross, who spoke beautiful Polish. She was a very lovely and affectionate person. She tried to win me over. She invited me to go with them to Zakopane; somehow she knew that I had dreamed of a trip such as this for a very long time. Zakopane was a beautiful town high in the Carpathian Mountains, and I always dreamed about going there for skiing in the winter or hiking in the summer. My mother agreed that I could go with them, and I went away for a week.

All through the week Mrs. Gross spoke to me about the Jewish religion. She explained some of the beautiful traditions that Jews celebrated. She bought me a blue dress to wear on Sabbath. On Friday night she lit candles and recited the blessings. My heart beat faster and faster. My eyes caressed this spectacle; I had such a warm, wonderful feeling. It was like nothing I had ever experienced before. I felt as though

the whole world had lit up in front of me. In this light I saw
the sun and the stars, and a bright future.

We climbed the mountains, and I was on top of the
world. Before I went home, Mrs. Gross invited me to come
to Belgium to stay with her and her two children. Belgium
sounded like a great, far away place; I begged my mother to
go with me. Mrs. Gross sent tickets for the two of us, and
we were treated royally when we arrived. Mr. Gross had
since grown back his beard and *peyos*, and returned to his
orthodox ways. He was a very gracious and polite host.

I was being pulled more and more into the Jewish religion, to Sabbath, and other observances, and my mother
began to worry. She saw how excited I was and how very
interested I was becoming in the Jewish religion, and one day
she asked me, "You are not planning to go back with me, are
you?" I was stunned. I didn't even realize how obvious my
involvement was; I was pulled, but didn't know it. I told my
mother that I wouldn't even think of staying here. I belonged
with her, and I'd return to Poland with her.

On a lovely summer day, I went for a walk in the park
with my mother and she spoke. "You know how much I love
you. I love you even more than my own daughter, but there
isn't much future for you in Poland. You know how difficult
life in Poland is for a Jew. You could never get into college,
and Mrs. Gross has helped you to apply to Stern College
already. I cannot interfere with your life anymore. Whatever
decision you make will be all right with me. We can visit each
other often."

My mind was spinning with confusion. I began to calcu-
late. How can I live without my mother? How can I leave her
alone? Where would I go? I began to cry and hugged my
mother. I told her that I would never leave her.

We walked home arm in arm. When we walked into the
house, Mrs. Gross was excited; she was yelling, "It worked!
It worked! Your application to college was accepted, and you
can go to Stern College in the biggest city in the world,
New York. You can study whatever you like," she said
breathlessly. "You received a scholarship, so you won't need

to worry about money. Your trip and everything else will be taken care of for you." My mother gasped with the news; she thought it was a miracle. She had dreamed of me going to college. She believed that I was too smart to work as a laborer. She wanted so much for me; she wanted me to be educated, to learn and to study, but she could never afford it. This was an opportunity that could not be ignored. My dear mother, she cried all night, and the next morning decided to return to Poland and leave me with these people. I cried when she left, but I think the thought of going to America sounded so great and so exciting that I was almost ready to chance it. But, as I soon learned, the road to freedom is never easy.

The day after my mother left, the whole family packed their belongings; we were all going to America, or so I thought. The plane took off from Antwerp and after forty-five minutes we landed. I looked questioningly at Mrs. Gross, hoping that she would explain this short flight, but she didn't say a thing. I was amazed. Finally I spoke: "Do you think I'm stupid? I'm eighteen years old; I have graduated from high school; I know that we can't be in America in forty-five minutes. Where are we?" I yelled. "What are you doing to me? What's happening?"

"We are in Geneva," Mrs. Gross told me. "We have to wait here for your visa to the US. We had to separate you from your mother; we had to take you away. We knew what you were going through, and we could see the anguish in your mother's eyes. Believe me, this will be the best for everybody, and the visas should reach here sooner. You'll have a wonderful time in Switzerland."

We drove to Montreux, where they had rented a house, but I was so miserable, I couldn't even appreciate the beauty of this country. I felt that I had committed a terrible injustice to my mother. I cried bitterly, and I couldn't understand how these nice people, religious people, could have done this to me. How could they have betrayed me so badly? For the next few days I sat in seclusion. I only talked to the children, never to Mr. or Mrs. Gross. Mrs. G. was desperate. She had tried so hard to make me understand, but nothing would do. I cried day and night. I felt so guilty and miserable.

Since the visas were taking so long, the Grosses finally decided we might just as well wait in Belgium. I accepted that idea, because I felt it would be closer to my mother. In October the whole family returned to Antwerp. Once we were home, the family demanded that I adjust to their ways. I was not allowed to do anything on Sabbath. I couldn't wear dresses with short sleeves, and I had to observe *kashrut*, the Jewish dietary laws. I had been a devout Catholic all my life, and all this was very difficult to comprehend and very strange for me. And yet, somehow, I was fascinated. Mrs. G. was a great teacher and evoked in me religious feelings I had never experienced before. I wanted to learn more and more. I was studying day and night. I went to Berlitz school and learned English. I lived a very religious life, and even though it confused me at times, I was eager to learn.

One day I met a girl who also had been hidden by a Polish family during the war. Unlike me, she had remained Catholic. I befriended her, and one Sunday the two of us went to church. I knelt and prayed, but something was missing. I kept remembering all the times I had gone to church with my mother, but this time I didn't find the inner peace, the contentment, that I had before. My heart wasn't in the prayer anymore. The words of other prayers, the Jewish prayers, were entering into my conversation with God. After I left the church, I knew that my heart and soul belonged to the Jewish religion, and it was time for me to stop fighting it. I became more active in Jewish life, and I began to enjoy it.

The whole Jewish community embraced me with open arms. I felt good; I felt I belonged, and I was more anxious than ever to find someone from my family, my Jewish family. I hoped that in America this too would be possible. When my mother came to visit me for a few days, she realized what had happened to me, and was ready to leave me, seeing how happy I was. I missed her after she left Belgium, but we wrote each other letters. Finally in August 1961 I wrote her a long letter, thanking her for everything she ever did for me, and telling her that I'd be leaving for America shortly.

Mrs. Gross accompanied me to New York. She found a place for me to live close to the university, and I began my studies. From the day I stepped off the plane I loved America. My road to freedom was very difficult and extremely long, but I had reached it. I had arrived.

I loved the people, I enjoyed studying, and I felt free. I started looking for some survivors from my family, and one day I learned that I had relatives in Detroit. They were cousins of my mother. They invited me to stay with them during the summer, and one Saturday at the temple, I met a young man who was also a survivor. It was love at first sight. In a few months we were married.

I was living a full and rich life in America, but my thoughts were very much with my Polish family. My love for my mother, the woman who brought me up, who sacrificed everything for me, never stopped. The memory of my Polish father, who was executed because he sheltered a Jewish child, will always be with me. My mother visited me in America many times before she died in 1986. I was at her bedside when she closed her eyes forever. During Christmas holidays in 1986, I went back to Poland and sang the carols with my adopted family. I lived a wonderful, religious, Jewish life, but the memory of the righteous Gentiles will forever live in my heart; I will forever be grateful.

Living in America has made me aware of the choices I have that my parents didn't have. I have the freedom to choose who I want to be and what I want to believe. My young mother had to give away her little baby to save her from imminent death. She couldn't save her five-year-old son—or herself—from the gas chambers of Auschwitz. I was fortunate to be saved. My parents weren't so lucky. Because of their selflessness and love, I now have the choices and the freedom that were denied them.

18. Mort Levy's Story: Saving Jewish Lives

Not all the people whose stories filled my head were survivors; some were Americans who helped us through those first dark days and years after the war. Morton Levy, from Allentown, Pennsylvania, played an integral part in my recovery. I first met him in Czechoslovakia; he was an officer in the American Army that liberated us. He was only a couple of years older than I, but his wisdom and his outlook on life were beyond his years. He helped us through our despair and almost convinced us that there was a bright future ahead of us.

My sisters and I first met Mort through Kurt, who befriended Mort on the streets of Prachatice. As Mort later told me, it struck him that here was a fourteen-year-old boy who would have died were it not for the presence of himself and the thousands of other American soldiers who had liberated the area. Mort was just twenty-three years old when he met Kurt, and the thought that he had played a part in saving a life was overwhelming to him.

Once in America, Henry and I continued to see Mort and his wife Myra. One summer I visited the Levys' home, and Myra shared with me a tape Mort had made describing his experiences in Europe. It was very difficult for him to talk about it, but finally one day he had to get it all out.

*　　*　　*

Nothing affected my life more than the act of a little boy who, extending his hand, with pleading eyes and without one spoken word, begged me to take him with me into the movie theater in Prachatice, Czechoslovakia, for the Saturday

146

matinee. What an adventure that day, my first Saturday in Czechoslovakia, started for me.

As in most theaters in the United States, the lobby had a candy counter. Naturally, I treated myself, and I filled both of the hands of my new little friend with all of the candy he indicated he wanted. No words were necessary to understand the passion he felt for that candy. Hand in hand, we slowly entered the dimly lit theater in search of two empty seats. No sooner had we settled into our seats when the movie started. In just a few moments, my newfound friend began to snuggle closer to me, and my instinctive reaction was to put my arm tenderly around his shoulder. I sensed that he felt comforted. When the picture was about half finished, I felt a tug on my arm. His inquisitive little face looked into mine as he asked me, *"Du bist a Yeed?"* ("Are you a Jew?") I was startled by the question. I answered yes. And so, as Humphrey Bogart said to Claude Rains in the final scene of the eternally famous picture *Casablanca*, this, too, was going to be the start of a beautiful friendship.

The month was August, and the year was 1945; World War II against Germany had been won. Before that successful conclusion, the 94th Infantry Division, of which I was a part, had occupied the coast of France in Brittany from St. Nazaire to Lorient. The mission of the 94th was to contain thousands of Nazis trapped in a successful fuel blockade. While our casualties were minimal during the period from September 1944 until December of that year, this relative tranquillity was brought to an abrupt halt when we were suddenly transferred east to the region at the German border known as the "Saar-Moselle Triangle." There the fighting was fierce and casualty rates high. In a historically short time, the Allies won complete victories in Belgium and Luxembourg, culminating in the dramatic victory of the Battle of the Bulge. We settled into the important industrial town of Krefeld, Germany. It was without difficulty that we crossed the Rhine River over pontoon bridges in our Jeeps, and made our headquarters in Düsseldorf. We were jubilant, as all successful armies are, especially on May 8, when V-E Day was pronounced, proclaiming the end of the war in Europe. The Allies had successfully waged war against the Third Reich. Hitler's reign of terror was finally at its end.

It is inconceivable in retrospect to understand the ignorance of the American GIs with regard to the Holocaust. Rumors had circulated that it was bad news to be a German prisoner of war, and it was desperately bad news to be a German prisoner of war if you were Jewish. We had heard of concentration camps, but they were regarded as camps that housed legitimate outspoken critics of the Third Reich such as Communists, unionists, and liberals. We had not begun to understand the magnitude of Germany's extermination programs against homosexuals, mentally retarded people, gypsies, and Jews. It was beyond imagination to conceive of such a vast slaughterhouse.

Our first visual contact with Nazi brutality was in Ohligs, near Düsseldorf. In the last days before Germany's surrender, seventy-one citizens of Ohligs suspected of harboring anti-Nazi sentiments were rounded up. They were forced to dig a common burial pit, were hog-tied with their arms behind their backs, shot in the back of the head, and buried just where they fell. One of our first political education acts while in Düsseldorf was to gather the entire population of Ohligs and make them bear witness to the opening of this stench-filled trench. In shock, they were made to see with their own eyes what had befallen their friends and neighbors of just a few days before. The Nazis were able to bury many vile acts, but their sins became more evident with each passing day.

These gruesome acts hit me in a particularly personal way because, as a Jew, I found it all too easy to see myself in the place of the victims. My own family had emigrated to New Jersey from Kiev sometime in the 1880s. As a second-generation American, I grew up with little sense of what it had been like in the old country, although I am told that until I was about five years old, I spoke Yiddish and English interchangeably, without understanding that there was a distinction.

My Jewish education was confined mostly to my child-hood. Until I was about ten, I wore *tzitzis*, the prayer shawl fringes worn by Orthodox male Jews as commanded in the Bible, but they had no religious significance to me; it was a thing done as naturally as wearing an undershirt. In those years I went to Hebrew school every day after having finished public school classes. It is downright shameful that I forgot practically everything that I ever learned.

Judaism faded somewhat into the background for me until I got my first view of silent and insidious antisemitism, at the University of Pennsylvania. I had obtained an athletic scholarship to Pennsylvania; and because I played varsity football and won the intramural heavyweight boxing champi-onship in my freshman year, the then all-Jewish fraternity, Tau Epsilon Phi, gave me a free membership. I soon learned that there were forty-three fraternities on the Pennsylvania campus. Thirteen of the forty-three fraternities were Jewish. The university labeled non-Jewish fraternities "Class A," and Jewish fraternities "Class B." Along with a small group of supporters (both Jewish and non-Jewish), I worked against this humiliating classification, and by the time I graduated, it had been abolished. Since then, to the credit of most colleges and universities, all fraternities have been desegregated on religious, ethnic, or racial grounds.

Although I had waged my own battle with institutional antisemitism, nothing could ever have prepared me for the grotesque and horrific consequences of the Nazis' version of it. This was attempted genocide, and I was glad to be able to play some part in stopping it.

Just as millions of other Americans, I had enlisted in the army a few days after Pearl Harbor. It was not because I was a hero, but more practically because I had already been classified 1-A by our Selective Service draft board. I knew that it was only a matter of time before I would be drafted. The Lord works in many mysterious ways, and this decision to enlist proved to be fortunate for me albeit by sheer accident. Immediately following my induction, indoctrina-tion, and various tests, I was told to report to the Army

Finance School at Fort Benjamin Harrison, Indiana. After intensive basic training and a four-month schooling program, far more rigorous and competitive than my four years at the Wharton School of Finance and Commerce, I was prepared to begin my duties as a finance officer in the U.S. Army.

I was fortunate because the finance department was always a part of a division's headquarters; during battle, even though we worked under rough, trying conditions, we were usually two to three miles to the rear of the actual lines of battle. The work was hard, demanding, and often complicated. Most of all, the department was in a constant state of crisis and confusion. But we in the department always gave thanks; we knew that we had an infinitely greater chance of survival than a combat infantryman. Another benefit of working at headquarters was that it gave me the opportunity to become rather closely acquainted with the generals of the division, the chief of staff, and other departmental chiefs. It would later prove helpful to have friends in high places, when I needed to prevent myself from being subjected to a potential court-martial. And this all came about because of that first fateful Saturday in Czechoslovakia, when a little boy reached out for a willing hand in search of a friend.

Many years and a continent away from my former life, I found myself sitting in this movie house with my new, young friend. By the end of the picture, I learned that his name was Kurt. I brought him with me to our quarters, and a group of friends and I outfitted him in a stray GI uniform; we adopted him as a sort of a mascot. The next day he managed to communicate to me that I should accompany him somewhere. When we arrived there, it was a large, old house and in it were six young girls. The oldest was Ruth and the sisters were Mania, Pola, and Anna. Two others, Lola and Gienia, were living with them, and Kurt had also been included in the group. From the outset it was obvious that Ruth was the strength and encouragement that enabled this group to survive. The younger ones did little else but cry, and it seemed that God provided Ruth with the wisdom and strength that translated their will to live into a reality. Despite the constant migraines that Ruth suffered, she stoically gave the necessary love and support to her younger charges.

A few days later, I introduced them to a soldier who occasionally had acted as cantor at the few Jewish services that we held. His name was Jack Kind, and he came from Brooklyn. I also introduced them to Phil Dorman, who was the aide-de-camp to Col. Earl Bergquist, the division's chief of staff. Between the three of us, we managed to confiscate better living quarters for the group. Through them we learned in vivid detail of the atrocities perpetrated by the Nazis on their victims.

Dorman, Kind, and I grew to love this collection of salvaged humanity. During this period when not on duty, our time was spent helping restore these children to a life in which they knew people loved and cared for them. They symbolized our own little special world, and somehow, we instinctively knew that we needed each other.

About September or October 1945, I was approached by someone who asked me to join a secret mission of mercy—with no questions asked. I was told only that it meant the future survival of many Jews. The mission, briefly described, was to "borrow" army trucks at night, and to appropriate the necessary fuel, food rations, and blankets to carry at least thirty people per truck. At a pre-arranged departure point, drivers would bring the trucks, load their human cargo, and head for a "westward destination." Most important, each vehicle had to be safely settled back into the motor pool before dawn. Through the help of Joe Fahy, an Irish friend of blessed memory who served in the office of the adjutant general, and the help of Lieutenant Rosenzweig in the quartermasters, the necessary supplies were obtained. Lt. Bennie Cohen, from Chicago, "took care of things" at the motor pool. This activity took place clandestinely for about three or four weeks. There was nothing more we were told, and nothing did we ask. It was much later that we learned we were a small part of a large underground helping to transport displaced persons to Palestine.

One day I was informed that the chief of staff wanted to

see me. We knew each other more than casually because we were both part of the initial cadre that served as the basis of the 94th Infantry Division. The chief's aide, my buddy Phil Dorman, cautioned me to be careful of every word I might speak. Naturally, I felt trepidation, not for myself, but because I was afraid that the chief had discovered what we had been doing. And, indeed, he had much more than a vague idea. But he was compassionate, understanding, and kind. In no uncertain terms he stated that "such activities must cease." He went on to warn me of the dire consequences that I might face if these activities continued. I guess it was pure *chutzpah*, the kind that comes from a mixture of fear and ignorance, that allowed me to request that I be granted a month to comply with his "command." I held my breath and waited for his reply. To my utter astonishment, he never said a word—in fact, he changed the subject entirely. I had been given the warm and friendly advice that was needed.

In the meantime things were happening so quickly around me. The atom bomb was dropped on Hiroshima; the Japanese surrendered, and overnight, the U.S. Army was ready to be dissolved. Soldiers with sufficient "service points" were being readied to return to civilian status. And I, like all the other GIs, was anxious to return home to my fiancée. It had been a long two years since I had seen her beautiful face.

In December 1945, I sailed from the port of Marseilles on the U.S. victory ship the *Zanesville*. Despite a terrible bout of sea sickness, I recall the thrill of watching the Statue of Liberty come into view as we arrived at New York Harbor. We were taken directly into Indiantown Gap, a separation camp in Pennsylvania; after signing scads of papers and finally receiving our discharge papers, we were formally returned to civilian status. Saluting everything in sight became just a memory.

On Christmas night, 1945, a cold and snowy night, I arrived at my parents' home in Allentown where Myra, my fiancée, was awaiting my arrival. No one ever received a better, warmer homecoming than I. As I think back, I realize how hard it must have been for parents and wives to have their children and spouses away at war. I believe that we, in the army, were much too young to worry and much too busy to care.

Myra and I were married soon after I arrived, and I was truly happy. I did, however, resolve to do whatever I could to save Jewish lives, restore Jewish dignity, and try to make my life meaningful and successful in the process. Fortunately, in all of those things, Myra and I shared common feelings and goals — and a willingness to forego other less important things.

Once I settled in, I got back to work and I was preoccupied and driven to get my life back in order. But each week, I put aside what I could from each paycheck, and once a month I sent a money order to Europe with the hope that one day it would help get survivors to America.

Unlike many stories, mine ends happily. Ruth, Mania, Pola, Anna, and even Gienia all came to the United States. Only Kurt, the little boy who changed my life, did not come. I was so happy when I heard that he had been reunited with his mother. He was one of the few lucky ones. My heart bleeds for all the other children who were killed, the children who never got the chance to grow and experience life.

*   *   *

I listened to the tape with tears in my eyes, and I was grateful to God for giving me the opportunity to live and to meet people like Mort Levy, who not only helped renew my strength, but helped me to build faith in humanity again. Mort and Myra Levy remained our friends; it is a friendship that has grown as only lifelong relationships can.

19. Dr. Faber's Story: Liberating Dachau

I often wondered, how much had the other American people known? Were any soldiers who served in the army prepared for what they found in German concentration camps? How could they comprehend? How could they ever understand what really happened? Rabbi Lipman once told me that he could not honestly say he hadn't known what was happening in Europe while he lived in America in peace and contentment before he was sent to war. He read the papers and heard the speeches; he knew Hitler was killing the Jews. And yet he couldn't really imagine it, didn't really even believe it until he saw it with his own eyes. I wondered if other Americans felt as he did.

One day I met Dr. S. Faber, an American doctor from Chicago whose unit had liberated Dachau, where thousands of people were exterminated. I was anxious to hear his story, and for days I listened to him as he related it slowly and emotionally.

*　　*　　*

I was a member of a medical unit of the U.S. Army. Our unit was stationed approximately twenty-five kilometers (fifteen miles) from Munich, Germany. On this sunny day in May 1945, we all knew that the war was over and we were jubilant. I was particularly exultant because I had enough points, after five years of active duty, to go home. My son, Jerry, had been born in November of the preceding year, and I had not yet seen him.

We all began to celebrate victory, but our celebration was

brought to a sudden halt when the commanding officer told us that our hospital, servicing the 45th Division, would immediately be moved to the concentration camp in Dachau. Where was Dachau? What were concentration camps? We had read about them in *Stars and Stripes*, the American newspaper for the troops. We had heard some rumors from other medical officers who joined us from other sections in Europe. Truthfully, though, we didn't know, nor did we understand, what it was all about. We were not prepared for what was ahead of us.

That same evening we began to move to Dachau, which we discovered was only a little distance from the battlefield. The camp was spread over a large area, many acres of land surrounded by barbed wire. Inside the camp were all kinds of prisoners, political and non-political, we were told. The first prisoners there had been mainly political detainees. Some were notables who were executed and some managed to escape—people like the sons of Stalin and Leon Blum (the former premier of France), and many others. Dissidents and intellectuals from all over Europe were eventually imprisoned in this camp.

When we arrived we were instructed by the officer in charge that our job was to treat as many of the inmates as possible. Several thousands were wounded, and we were to take care of these first. I do not know the exact numbers. We were never able to count them, but at one time there had been as many as thirty thousand prisoners in Dachau. I guess there were still about ten to twelve thousand when we arrived.

The end of the war had come most quickly and unexpectedly to the SS officers who were guards and administrators of this camp. Those unable to flee or to escape before the Americans came to liberate the camp quickly changed into concentration camp uniforms and pretended to be prisoners. The camp uniforms were zebra-striped, blue and white, similar to the uniforms in our U.S. prisons. The inmates, half-alive, knew their persecutors well. Our American soldiers, who were shocked and horrified at what they saw when they entered Dachau, handed their rifles to the inmates, who could hardly stand up. These poor souls nonetheless held the guns and shot the SS men in their midst. When our unit arrived at the camp, there were dead SS men all over the place.

I remember there was graffiti all over the camp that was later translated for us by some of the inmates. Hitler's ideology was scribbled on the camp walls: "All human culture, all art and sciences were the exclusive products of the Aryan culture." Or: "The Aryan stock and only the Aryan stock is the biological species, with the characteristic shape of the scalp, with a specific tint of complexion, and the proper blood. Non-Nordic man is closer to an animal than to the human race. To suppress and to destroy the non-Nordic men and specifically the Jews is an elevated destiny to be reached by the pursuit and sacrifice to the end, to the complete destruction."

It was a warm, sunny morning outside when we all were assigned a ward. There were approximately two of our medical personnel assigned to every hundred beds. The beds were made of canvas, easily assembled, and we traveled with them all through Europe. Supplied with nurses, medication, intravenous fluids, and every medical treatment the U.S. Army possessed, we went to work.

When my crew and I arrived at ward number twenty, we all froze. My first thoughts: "Are all these people Jewish? How can I recognize a Jewish person? The names on the cards are illegible. What can I say? How can I speak with them?" All were like living skeletons, dehydrated and cadaverous victims lying there, fecal matter all over their beds. Sanitation was non-existent, and the stench was unbearable. It was impossible to think straight. I felt so depressed and helpless that I felt like running, and yet I had an urgent desire to tell them that I was also Jewish, that I felt for them, that I wanted to help. I finally decided I'd simply say, "I'm Jewish. I'm a Jew, Yiddish, from America."

You can't imagine what happened when I uttered those words. They couldn't even lift their heads. Their bodies were afflicted with typhus, ulcerations, tuberculosis, and many other diseases, but the expression on their faces was all the body language they needed. *"Ratove meehr, ratove meehr"* ("Save me, help me"), they begged over and over again, their hands held out to me in supplication. Naturally I was overjoyed at their reaction and tried to reach them in a mixture of Yiddish and German, assuring them that they would be taken care of medically, that they would be given food and shelter, and repatriated as soon as possible.

The feelings that went through me were unimaginable. These helpless victims were grabbing my hands, crying on my shoulder, pulling on my clothes, weeping heavily, and asking questions. And all I could do was try to soothe their pain and take care of their wounds. I kept assuring them that the war was over, and they had nothing to fear anymore, but I saw fear in their eyes for a long, long time.

We were able to locate some secret files from which we learned that there were physicians from Bulgaria, Hungary, and Yugoslavia who had been saved from the gas chambers because at the end of the war the SS needed them, not for the inmates, but for their own ills. They were former prisoners and only they knew what had really happened in Dachau. They wanted us to take the camp records and listen to their stories so that we could tell the world.

These doctors related tales that made me physically ill. We heard stories of sadistic experiments. The Nazis would make prisoners drink exorbitant amounts of water until severe complications resulted, or they'd submerge someone in a tub of ice water, constantly lowering the temperature below freezing to determine how long the person could survive. Those who refused to do the experiments were shot. Operations on female reproductive organs were done constantly. Other experiments had to do with natural bodily functions. They would not allow a group of men and women to urinate or defecate for long periods of time, until the people collapsed and died. Castrations and sterilizations were performed on thousands. These files were kept so that people could never forget or deny.

Meanwhile, we worked day and night trying to save as many lives as we could. Sickness was rampant. All kinds of diseases, many unknown to us, were spreading among the survivors. We had plasma, blood, and all possible medications, but of course, some of the inmates we treated were too far gone to survive. Their kidney functions had diminished to the point of failure, and heart diseases were beyond our control. Those who were able to leave the hospital were repatriated to their own countries, that is, all except the Jews. There was no country that would take them. I often wondered what happened to them. Their images are always before my eyes, their whispers—"save me, help me"—always bring a pain into my heart.

The tragedies of the Holocaust caused an eruption on this earth more shattering than any previous experience. The Germans raised themselves to heights of power that had never been known before. They built Germany on the ashes of millions of people whose lives they extinguished. My mind still refuses to comprehend that such savagery occurred in our lifetime. I'll forever ask questions.

*   *   *

I'll never forget this wonderful doctor, who helped so many deathly ill people at Dachau to survive and to recover. Fortunately, there were many devoted Americans who gave of their time and even sacrificed their lives to bring these people out of hell and into freedom.

Part Four
Free at Last

20. *America, the Goldeneh Medina*

We are going to America! The thought echoed in our minds and hearts, and yet it was so hard to believe it. Ellen was almost two years old and she couldn't understand much about what was happening. Mommy and Daddy were taking her far, far away, over the mountains and over the ocean to a new and wonderful land: America. She repeated it many times and was eager to tell all her dolls and her teddy bear that she was taking a long journey by boat.

Her tiny hands were busy collecting her treasures and her beautiful blue eyes were smiling. She couldn't understand why *"liebe* Gertrud" had to stay behind, but we explained that Gertrud had to take care of another little girl. Gertrud had been taking care of Ellen since the day she was born. Despite my initial trepidation about having a German nurse-maid, God had been good to me, for Gertrud had proved to be a wonderful "nana" to my dear Ellen. "Ellen must have fresh air no matter what the weather," she would insist. I can still see my little darling walking out in her raincoat and hood. She was a perfectly healthy baby who never gave us any trouble. She seemed to be excited about this new adventure—going to America with Mommy and Daddy.

The rocking ship couldn't compare with the rocking chair, and unfortunately both she and I were sick all the way across the ocean. In moments when she felt a little better, we would watch the roaring ocean through the round window. It was difficult for her to understand that we were far away from everything she had ever known, and she spent a lot of time searching the ocean for *liebe* Gertrud. A few days before we left, Gertrud had written in her diary: *"Ellen klein geht allein in die weite Welt hinein"* ("Little Ellen goes alone into the big wide world").

Our hearts were heavy for we were leaving behind the unknown graves of our parents, my brother, and many friends and relatives who had perished during the war. Since the Lord had granted us the greatest gift of all—life—we were taking it now to this new country, America. It was with great pride that Henry and I looked at our most treasured possession, this little girl, our only child. We wanted so much to build a new life for her and around her.

The voice of the captain sounded loud and clear: "We have now reached the shores of the United States of America. Helloooooo . . ."

The long, stormy journey was over.

When we finally reached the city of New York, my eyes were dancing up to the tall buildings and down to the millions of people—people everywhere! At first I couldn't imagine that so many people had survived the war. I thought that Hitler had killed everybody. It took me quite a while to realize that these people had hardly been touched by the war. This is another continent, I reminded myself. Certainly there were all those wonderful young men who fought Hitler, who fought this war, or otherwise I wouldn't be here. They were the ones who liberated us, who gave us freedom. But the others, the ones who stayed home. . . Do they know? Will they ever know?

I watched the people hurry in the streets. They hurried here, they hurried there. I wondered why they were rushing. What were they thinking? One thing that always puzzled me was that they didn't actually know each other. In Poland, in my own town, everybody knew everybody. But here they didn't know each other, and yet I walked in the street and a complete stranger said, "Hi, how are you?" I liked that, but what should I do? Should I answer? Should I tell her that I'm so amazed at this new world? Or maybe I should tell him that I'm a foreigner and that I feel utterly lost in this big city. Or perhaps I should just pretend and say, "Thank you, I feel well." Very soon I too started greeting everybody, "How are you?" Some answered "fine," but others gave me funny looks.

I believe the thing that impressed me most in the first few days in this big city were the fruit stands. Green, red, orange, yellow, large and small, fruits I had never seen before, smells I had never smelled. My teeth were anxious to crunch each and every one. I wanted the flavor of all these fruits to seep into my throat. If only I could afford to buy some of these fruits. If only I could taste their delicious flavor. Perhaps one day. . . .

For several months we lived in one small room at a hotel assigned to us by the American Joint Distribution Committee, who had also sponsored our trip. We took our meals in a restaurant next door. With all my knowledge of the English language, I realized that I didn't know the names of foods. Everything on the menu looked strange. There was one thing, however, that was familiar: "spareribs with sauerkraut." We knew sauerkraut from Germany. Since our budget was extremely limited, we couldn't afford to experiment, so every night the three of us would sit down to a dinner of spareribs and sauerkraut. Poor Ellen made faces, but she too got used to this meal.

The room in the hotel was so small that there was hardly any place for Ellen to play, and when it rained the three of us had to sit on our beds. Life was becoming unbearable. We often wondered if it had all been worth it. What was this freedom all about? America was supposed to be the *goldeneh medina*, the golden land, where the streets were paved with gold. But we seemed to be worse off now than we had been in Germany. The nightmares kept us awake half the night; the days without work, without activity of any sort were becoming impossible.

Little Ellen was growing up, and she needed more space. She needed friends. We knew that we had to find a place to live if we were going to go on living at all. We had no money left; the few dollars we had brought with us were used for food, and we had to turn to someone for help. We contacted the Jewish Agency in Brooklyn, because we heard that they were helping our people. Sure enough, they found a furnished room for us in Brooklyn. We had a bedroom, and we shared the living room and kitchen with the young man who owned the place.

Once we were settled into our new place, Henry walked over to St. Joseph Hospital, which was very close to where we lived, and applied for an internship in medicine. He had to study English day and night to pass the English exam, and as soon as he passed this test, he had to study again for his medical boards. At least he was occupied and could use some of the hospital rooms for his studies.

Henry would take the bus to work. His salary was fifty dollars a month—less than a taxi driver's wages—which was hardly sufficient for three people to live on. Desperate for some extra money, he would take ambulance calls, which paid fifty cents per patient. My budget was so limited that my brain worked overtime to try to figure out the best way to use the little money we had to buy food for the three of us. Our struggle for survival continued.

The fortunate thing was that as soon as we settled in Brooklyn, Ellen made a lot of friends. At first she found it very difficult to communicate with the children because she only spoke German. "Mommy, tell me what they say?" she would ask. Mommy translated for her, played with her, took her for long walks in the park, and told her stories.

The second winter came and Ellen could speak English fluently. Mommy was expecting a baby. What a thrill, she would have her own baby, Ellen said. "I will be the big sister. I will wheel the carriage and take care of my baby sister." She was so excited; she shared her joy with all her friends. She explained to them that when the trees turned green, and the flowers bloomed, the baby would arrive and she would be very happy.

Spring came and the baby was born. It was a little sister for Ellen, and we called her Vivian Ann. Ellen rocked her little baby sister to sleep; she sang to her, and very soon she even tried to feed her. She slept in the same room with the baby and Mommy and Daddy, and was truly helpful and busy for her young age.

We all were busy, and time passed quickly. Taking care of two children, the house, the cooking, and the cleaning took the better part of my days. When night came and Henry walked in, I was utterly exhausted and hardly had the strength to feed him and stay up with him. I was emotionally and physically drained.

Oh, God, how I wished that my sisters could be with me at times like that.

21. Reunited with My Sisters

Fortunately all my sisters were in America already. Since we were all sponsored by the American Joint Distribution Committee, we had no choice about which American city we would end up in, and as it happened we all had to go to different cities. We were not really far from each other—we were all on the eastern seaboard—but without a car or money for public transportation, our visits were very limited.

One Sunday morning, a friend of Henry's drove us to Providence, Rhode Island, to visit Mania and her husband Sam and to see her little baby. We were overjoyed to see each other, and I was especially glad to see my little niece, who had been born after they got to America and whom we had therefore never seen. Mania and I finally got a chance to catch up on each other's lives since crossing the ocean.

She told me about her first impressions of New York when they arrived; they had taken a taxi into the city at rush hour. "There must have been thousands of cars moving in all directions," she said, "or at least it seemed that way to me. I had never in my life seen anything like that. I thought that this was a parade. I believed that America was greeting us. I believed that because they knew how much we had suffered, they wanted to show us how much they cared. I waved to all of them. I looked out my window and wanted to yell to them, to thank them for everything, to tell them how happy I was to be alive and in America!"

She spoke, too, of the strangeness of adjusting to life in another country, and of getting to know her new neighbors in Providence, who, although not unkind, had treated Sam and Mania as curiosities. "I couldn't imagine what these people expected to see after they'd heard stories from Germany," Mania told me. "They knew that some Jews survived the atrocities and were coming to America to live. But from what they'd heard, they couldn't imagine the survivor to be a normal human being. They were amazed at everything they learned about us. They thought we would be wild, especially about food; they thought we would be forever grabbing for something to eat. When they came into my house and saw the table set for dinner, they couldn't believe it. When Sam found a job in a store and went to work every day dressed as well as we could afford, they were amazed. It was a long time before these people realized that we could live the same kind of life they did."

Most poignant of all, though, was when Mania told me about the birth of her baby daughter. She had been eight months pregnant when they arrived in the U.S. A month later, far away from me and our other sisters, she entered the hospital at night and had her daughter the next morning. "I was afraid to touch the baby," Mania confided. "I didn't want to take it in my arms. In my mind babies had to be killed. No Jewish baby had the right to live. I couldn't imagine that I could keep this baby. Every day the doctor came and told me I could go home. He assured me that the baby was doing fine, and that I could now take care of her by myself, but I wouldn't go home. I was so scared! After two weeks in the hospital, Sam finally made me go home.

"He called a neighbor to come pick us up. I came home with the baby, and I was so lonely. Mother wasn't there to comfort me. You and Pola and Anna weren't there to help me. Sam left for work every day, and I was alone. My nightmares came back, and I started thinking again about Mother being taken from us at Auschwitz, about how I had always thought we could have saved her, even though I know there was really nothing we could have done. Fortunately, some of my neighbors were coming to see me and to help me. I befriended a couple of them and I began to feel better. With their help, I was beginning to learn how to take care of my baby, and I enjoyed it more and more. I think once I reconciled with this little creature and believed that she was mine, my life started to change. I've started taking walks with her, talking to her, and cuddling her; I'm finally beginning to live."

I was so glad to hear her story and to know that she was doing well. I was also glad that she had confided in me; I always believed that talking about the past makes it easier for the survivor to live with. For some it is absolutely impossible to talk about, however. One of those people who has chosen not to talk about the past is my sister Pola. She and her husband Dolek were settled on Long Island with their twin boys. Henry and I occasionally went out to visit them, but Pola and I kept to discussions of the present, never the hell that was our past.

My life had been and always will be intertwined with my sisters, but the one who is closest to me is my youngest sister Anna. She arrived in America a couple of months before I did, and had a very difficult time making a living. She had arrived in New York with no money and had to look for a job immediately. She had no job experience, and her English was poor, so she went to night school. She found a job sewing in a factory. The first week, she made all of eight dollars, but as her boss handed her the check, he propositioned her and frightened her out of her wits. With her eight dollars, she bought a ticket to Binghamton, New York, where Uncle Jack and Gienia were living. But she couldn't find a job there and had to hitch a ride back to New York without a penny to her name. She was faced with looking for another job, and was convinced the only way to get one was to be "nice" to the boss. Fortunately, she met some survivors who lived in New Jersey, and they invited her to move in with them. She shared a room with the two girls and found herself a job as a waitress.

Anna had been waitressing for a short time when Mark walked in, the man she had met and fallen in love with in Stuttgart! They were overjoyed to find each other again, and were married after a few months. Mark had been a lawyer in Poland, but in order to get work in the U.S. as a lawyer, he would have to go back to school, which they couldn't afford. So the two of them took whatever jobs they could find to put food on the table.

Anna was having trouble getting pregnant; she had never menstruated during the war, and it was years before her system began to work. It never really worked properly, though. Her health in general left a lot to be desired. She had been only nine years old when the war started, and her growing years were spent in concentration camps. Besides her health problems, Anna was suffering from terrible nightmares during this time. She couldn't stop thinking about the past, reliving it night and day with unbelievable clarity. She couldn't sleep, couldn't function. Finally, she went for psychiatric help. Eventually she found a doctor who could remove the tattoo from her arm. She no longer wanted the numbers put there in Auschwitz that served as a reminder. She didn't want to talk about the past any more, or think about it, either.

Jack and Gienia felt the same way. They were settled in Binghamton now with their son, trying to start a new life with a positive outlook. Jack went to night school and learned English. He was a furrier and was able to get a job in a large department store. There were very few survivors in Binghamton, but Jack and Gienia had no trouble making friends with Americans. The people in the community were very nice to them.

It was not easy adjusting to life in this new country, but my sisters and I were all making progress, getting settled in, and doing the best we could.

22. *My Little Girl Is Gone*

On December 31, 1951, we were going to celebrate Ellen's fourth birthday. She was going to have a party, and all her friends and our neighbors were invited. There were little hats for the children, and baskets with candy for everyone. Everything was prepared, but there was to be no party.

Every morning when Ellen woke up she would come to our bed and kiss us good morning. On this morning she didn't come in to see us. Henry was concerned. "Go see what's wrong with Ellen," he said. I went into her room. She had her eyes wide open, but she didn't look right.

"What's the matter, darling?" I asked. My hand reached for her forehead; she was burning up with fever. I took her temperature and it was 105. I yelled for Henry to come quickly. He looked at her and rushed to the telephone to call the doctor, a friend of ours. The doctor came over in no time, examined Ellen, and took a sample of her blood. He was very apologetic, but he thought it better to be cautious and check everything out. He suggested that it could be a simple cold, but joked that with a doctor's child you always have to look for something unusual, fancy blood counts and all.

"Mommy, I don't like this doctor. I want Daddy," Ellen protested.

"Don't worry, darling," I soothed her. "This doctor will make you feel all better, and Daddy will take care of you."

The blood was checked, and we received a phone call telling us to come to the doctor immediately. We went together hand in hand, Henry and I. Not in my wildest dreams did I have any doubts but that it was just a simple cold or some viral infection. The expression on Henry's face and the look in his eyes worried me, though. He looked positively frightened.

The doctor was telling us about the blood count not being so good. He wanted us to admit Ellen to the hospital so he could run more tests. I was utterly confused. This baby was perfectly well yesterday. She was playful; she was looking forward to her birthday party. How could we do this to her? How could we take her to the hospital? The doctor must be mistaken, I thought. I'll keep her home. I'll give her good care, and she will be better in a couple of days. I said as much to the doctor, and he looked at me strangely. "Why is he looking at me that way?" I wondered. "What's the matter with Henry, anyway? Why doesn't he say something?"

"Come on, honey," I said to Henry. "She will be home with us. You'll take care of her and we'll give her everything she needs at home."

The doctor spoke rather sternly: "My dear Ruth, I'm afraid there isn't much you can do for her at home. She will be much better off at Mount Sinai Hospital in New York. We need to run some more tests, and only they can do what is necessary for your child."

"Well, if you really think that we have to bring her to the hospital . . . if it's better for her?" I whispered.

"I think we'd better take her," Henry said as he reached for my hand. He looked longingly at the doctor as if to say, "Please tell my wife what's wrong with our child."

"I can't really say for sure what is wrong," the doctor began, "but the blood tests show a large number of white cells, and it seems likely that Ellen is suffering from a very serious illness. It's called leukemia," he said, looking very sadly at Henry and me.

This doctor must be wrong, I thought. He simply can't tell me that my darling, my beautiful child is sick, very sick. It can't happen to me, to her. Somebody tell me it's not true. My mind could not comprehend; I only wanted to escape this reality. I wanted to hide from it, deny it, but I had no place to turn, and nobody to run to. I only wished my mother could be with me. She would know what to do.

I walked home in a daze. The baby was crying in her crib and little Ellen was lying in bed, still burning with fever. I asked my neighbor, who had been staying with the children, to watch Vivian while we took Ellen to Mount Sinai Hospital. "Darling, Mommy and Daddy must take you to the hospital," I explained to Ellen. "The doctors need to run some tests and they can only do it there. But I'll be with you, my love, don't you worry. We'll come back home soon and you can play with your little sister." I kissed her and fought back the tears. I dressed her in her best clothes, and together Henry and I took her for the long, long ride.

"Look, darling, this is the Brooklyn Bridge." Henry was trying to distract his little girl. "Now we'll go over the bridge, a long, long bridge; and when we come back, we'll cross the same bridge again, and we'll be back home!" he explained.

We arrived at the hospital. It was a big building with a lot of elevators and long corridors. We got Ellen settled into her bed; we tried to comfort her. Then the moment came when we had to leave Ellen and go home. How do you leave a child? How could we leave our dearest daughter? I suddenly felt that if I left her, it would be just like it had been in Europe, where innocent little children were killed. I was consumed by a terrible fear.

I looked at my child. I looked at Henry, and suddenly I realized where I was. This is America, for goodness sake, I reminded myself. I'm in America now. This is one of the best hospitals in the country, where they cure people, not kill them. Henry took one look at me and recognized the fear in my eyes. He kissed me tenderly. "Please, my dear," he whispered, "let's see what will happen. Let's wait until tomorrow. They will run more tests."

I wished tomorrow would never come, but it did.

In a small conference room Henry and I were told that our child had the most dreaded disease of all, and there was no cure. She had leukemia. The doctor explained in detail the function of the blood and the treatments and disturbances to be expected. He found it necessary, however, to tell us that there wasn't much hope. Ellen's case was in the acute stage.

How does a parent accept such news? More so, how does a father who is a physician, whose life is supposed to be dedicated to healing people, reconcile himself to the fact that he cannot save the life of his own child?

How does he go on living?

I turned to prayer. I believed that where there is life, there is hope, and I couldn't imagine that God would want to take this child away from me.

And so I prayed, and I hoped. There were several critically ill children on this ward; we played with them, brought them toys, and our hearts were breaking. We never left the hospital. We had taken Vivian to stay with my sister Pola, who took care of her for the next two months. Vivian played with Pola's twin sons, and I hoped that she would be all right. I couldn't leave Ellen. Henry and I stood next to her bed throughout her entire illness. The nurses wouldn't even let us take a chair to sit next to her. During the night they wouldn't let us stretch out on the couch in the waiting room. The staff's behavior was horrible beyond description. I will never understand it.

Ellen was failing rapidly, and one day we decided to give her the birthday party she had missed. She wore a dress and the children were singing, but she was too weak to sing. I prayed to God to give me strength to laugh and to look happy, so she wouldn't see me cry. She asked for some special toys, and we desperately wanted to give her everything she asked for, but we didn't have any money.

One day I stopped for a cup of coffee and told the storekeeper that my little girl was very ill, and she dreamed about a merry-go-round toy, but I couldn't afford it. The next day he sent a beautiful merry-go-round to the hospital for my Ellen. She was barely able to move her hands now. She realized that she was very sick, but she still talked about going home to her sister.

As long as she was breathing we had hope. The world

was working on research for leukemia; maybe something would be found. Henry called all the doctors he could, asking for advice, for help, for a few months of life for his little girl. Two months passed and nothing could be done. I sat next to her and prayed to God: "Please, God, don't let her suffer so." The injections she received didn't give her much relief anymore. She belonged to another world. If only the Lord would take her and spare her suffering.

I'm losing her, I'm losing this child. Her body is still near, but not her soul. This incurable disease they call leukemia has consumed her body step by step. Her little hands reach out to me: "Mommy, I love you, help me, Mommy, please help me. I don't want to hurt anymore."

My eyes reach out to heaven, and my silent prayers turn to God, but there is no help from anywhere. Very soon her heart stops beating, her soul reaches up to the skies to join the angels in heaven. My child lost the struggle with death because of a terrible disease for which mankind had not found a cure. My little girl is gone. She is dead.

I gave a terrible, inhuman cry that shook the hospital walls. I wailed for hours. My child was gone forever.

There was no cure for leukemia and no miracle for my child. She lay dead at the young age of four. One more soul among the millions who died in the Holocaust. Was she also a victim of war? Was it the "herbs" I had been given in the concentration camps to dry up my menstruation? Was it the medication I received when I was in a German hospital during my pregnancy? Was it my past that caused her to die?

On February 29 (the leap year), 1952, we buried our Ellen in a distant cemetery in Queens, New York. Our dearest friend, Rabbi Eugene Lipman, who was now a rabbi in a temple in New York City, found a grave for our child. We had no money to buy a burial plot, but he got his congregation to cover all the costs of the funeral. Once again Rabbi Lipman gave us his support. I had conducted funerals with him before, in Europe. Now he was helping me to bury my own child.

My sisters all came to the funeral with their spouses.

When we came together at this tragic time in our lives, all the sadness, all the pain of losing our family members came to the surface; the pain demanded a response. This time we could come together and bury our loved one; this time we could say good-bye. Finally we were able to mourn for those we had lost; finally we were able to shed the tears that had been hidden for so long. Ellen's death brought all these feelings out, and we all felt so close again.

After the funeral, Henry and I went with Pola and Dolek to their house to see our little baby Vivian. When we walked into the apartment, Vivian stood up in her crib and uttered her first word: "Dada." Henry looked at her, turned around, and left the room crying hysterically. For many years, whenever he looked at Vivian, he would start crying for Ellen. He took the loss terribly. She was his little girl. He suffered as a doctor because he had been unable to help her. The guilt was eating him up. I had to function for Vivian, for this little child God had given me. I had to survive the loss and go on living for the little treasure who was in my arms.

From that moment on, I began to feel in a new way the loss of the million and a half children who were killed during the war. I felt for all the mothers. I knew now what an indescribable pain it was to lose a child. I realized that a part of me had died again.

We returned to our apartment in Brooklyn, but every step, every corner, reminded us of Ellen. We knew we had to leave this place if we were to go on living. Within the next two months we moved into a new section in Queens called Kew Gardens. Vivian had a tiny room, just enough space for a crib, and we had a bedroom, a living room, and a small kitchen. We borrowed money from everybody we could, hoping that Henry would soon be able to work again and we'd be able to repay our debts.

Henry mourned Ellen terribly. He would take the subway to the cemetery and stay there for hours. He had quit working. "If I couldn't help my child, how can I help others?" he would say. He stayed home and read books and cried. During Ellen's illness we had communicated, we had

175

strengthened each other; we needed each other so badly, and our love was intensified by this need. But now, since we had lost her, we couldn't communicate anymore. We couldn't talk about her; we couldn't share our pain. We were so lonely in our suffering.

Unfortunately, our attitude also affected Vivian. She developed all kinds of allergies, rashes all over her body, and all kinds of sicknesses. We took her to a doctor, and one day after he examined her, he told us that something was definitely wrong with her blood. We almost lost our minds. We paced the room all night. The next morning the doctor called and told us that the changes in her blood were caused by the infection she had, and she would be all right in a couple of days. This one-year-old child had suffered her sister's death in so many ways.

In the spring of 1953, I made a decision: Henry and I had to start all over again. We must start anew. He must leave the city and the cemetery. We must leave this home and this area, and we must begin a new life once more. We rented a car and drove through New York State.

23. To Live Again

It was May 1953. We left New York early in the morning. We were on our way to Syracuse, New York, where we had learned the medical society was in search of more doctors. Since Binghamton was on our way, we stopped and spent a nice day with my uncle Jack and his wife Gienia and their two little boys (they had had a second son since we had seen them last). Jack and Gienia offered to take care of Vivian while we went to Syracuse to check out the situation. She seemed to be happy with the boys, so we left her there.

Henry and I drove quietly without a word.

Our eyes were filled with the world around us. As we looked through the windows of the car, we could see the rolling hills; we could see the rich, green leaves on the trees; we could even see the flowers beginning to bloom. The car windows were wide open, and we breathed in the fresh air, cleansing our lungs and soothing our pain. We were awakening to spring, to life.

It had been so long since I had heard a bird sing. How strange that this was always the first thing I noticed. Whenever I was imprisoned, in camps or simply in my heart, I closed my ears to the world outside. And yet nature was such an integral part of my life. One couldn't help it, being born in a small village at the foot of the Carpathian Mountains. One lived in nature. I climbed the mountains from the time I was able to walk. I always picked my own bouquets of flowers, and I still do that wherever I live. I remember the chirping and the singing of the birds, and trying to imitate them as soon as I could utter a word. Bu the birds did not sing for me when I was sad. Not even the mourning dove who could always move me, not the woodpecker who made my heart pound. I couldn't hear the birds when my heart was heavy.

And now, I listened to the birds as we drove through New York State, and I looked at Henry and he looked at me, and I knew then for the first time since Ellen's death that there was still something left between us. There was enough love between us to help us overcome this tragedy together.

We stopped at a rest area. Henry took me in his arms and his lips were warm, his kisses sweet. We held hands and looked at the valley below us, and it felt good. We watched the greening of the trees and the birds flying above, and it was good. We could smell spring in the air and feel the warmth of the sun above, and it was good. We greeted spring as if we were greeting a new life.

We arrived in Syracuse. We didn't know a soul. We had no idea what to expect, but we felt good. We found the medical society office, and a very pleasant fellow greeted us. He was happy to show us around and to point out all kinds of places available for doctors' offices. He tried to sell us on the idea of settling in a village outside the city where doctors were desperately needed, but I wanted to be in the city. I wanted a neighborhood school for my children, and I also wanted to be surrounded by a Jewish community. I wanted to attend services at a synagogue, and I wanted my children to learn about Judaism. I was really aching for contact with people, and I was still afraid that the non-Jewish people wouldn't accept us.

We had no money. The gentleman from the medical society found a place where a doctor wanted to sell his practice and his home so he could retire to Arizona. The doctor agreed to sell us the house with mortgage payments to him starting in a few months. We didn't even know that we could go to a bank and apply for a mortgage, possibly at a lower rate. We didn't know America.

The house was over a hundred years old. The attic had beautiful stained glass windows, and the garden had some pretty flowers. The office downstairs was adequately furnished. Up the old stairway was a bright, comfortable apartment. This was to be our first real home in America. We rushed to Binghamton, picked Vivian up, and then went back to Kew Gardens to close our place there and move all our belongings to Syracuse.

I looked at my Vivian and my heart felt good. I looked at Henry and he seemed happy. He had a smile on his lips for the first time in a long, long time. He hugged me and kissed little Vivian. God help him, I prayed. He had been depressed for such a long time and in so many ways. Now was his time, his time to work, his time to provide for his family, and perhaps his time to find a new faith, faith in God, faith in himself. Day by day I could see the difference in him. He would jump out of bed in the morning and rush downstairs to his office where patients were already waiting. In no time, he built a wonderful practice and his patients loved him. He was a real practitioner. They came to him with all their troubles, physical or psychological. Through the years they came to love and respect him, and he felt good.

In the beginning he even delivered babies, and every baby he delivered was in a way replacing his lost child. He was invigorated by his work. He was so involved with medicine, with healing, with curing, that sometimes I felt I was dealing with a new man. Something very strong was growing between the two of us. Our longing for each other was so great that we couldn't wait to be together, if only for short moments. It was in those days that I felt true love; I felt a desire I had never felt before. I knew then that nothing, but nothing, would shake our love again. Henry was so busy with his work that we had very little time together, but our love was greater than ever. I knew that we had survived the war to be together.

The fall in upstate New York was a dream come true. The leaves were turning brilliant yellows, oranges, and reds. The autumn flowers were in bloom, and the birds were enjoying their familiar territory for the last few months before they would head south. Our little girl was beginning to walk and talk. Her laughter filled our house and our hearts. But when Henry looked at Vivian he would cry for the firstborn daughter he missed so much. I felt we needed spiritual guidance, and we went to see the local rabbi. Rabbi Irving Hyman understood our pain. He had been a chaplain during the war, like our friend Rabbi Lipman, and he knew where we had come from. He helped us to enter the religious community, and he guided our way to God and to faith. He had long talks with Henry and helped him to come to some acceptance of Ellen's death. Slowly Henry began to find comfort and relief in prayer. He would go with me to temple, and he would even pray at home on his days off.

On October 30, 1954, I gave birth to our son, Jeffrey Dan. For nine months I prayed and hoped that it would be a boy. I was so scared that if I had another girl, Henry would see Ellen in her. When my doctor delivered the baby and announced, "It's a boy," I closed my eyes in thanks, and I knew then that I could trust God with all my heart and soul.

Our little boy came at such a wonderful time in our lives. He brought so much joy. Henry was playing with a baby for the first time since Ellen's death. He took time to be with him and to hold him. It was like Henry had returned after a long absence. He was born again; he had energy now, and a desire to move forward rather than to dwell in the past. His relationship with our Vivian slowly changed. She stopped being scared of him; she didn't see his tears anymore. That encouraged him, and he began to play with her also. He let her hold her little brother, and he talked to her. It felt to me as if another miracle had happened. We all communicated with each other. We felt close. We knew that we had each other and could overcome anything.

Lying in bed at night, I remembered Henry's mother's last wish for us before she went to the gas chambers of Auschwitz. I was sure that she knew we were together. I was sure that she watched over us, and I was at peace with myself. I looked forward now to another sunrise, another morning. . . .

Epilogue

I was quite busy keeping house and taking care of my two
little ones. But when they were old enough, I enrolled them
in a nursery school where they could be with other children.
I had to find some work for myself. I knew that I wanted to
work with children, to teach them what hatred can do, and
to help them build a better world for themselves and for
future generations. In the early fifties and sixties, there were
more and more African-Americans coming to town. There
was a tremendous need for volunteers, and being a newcomer
myself, I could understand their needs. The Syracuse high
schools had a big problem with dropouts because these young
people wanted to find work and make a living instead of
staying in school. They didn't feel the need for education.
For the next ten years I worked with an organization called
Youth Opportunities Unlimited, which would help to stimu-
late young people to stay in school. I went from being a
secretary to becoming president of the organization. I
worked with all my heart and soul to help these young
people, and every time one of them finished high school, or
better yet went on to college, I was triumphant.

In the sixties I also worked with Jewish youth groups. I
started new groups and organized all kinds of activities for
young people. I was involved. I was learning and I was
sharing my experiences with others. I also went to school and
got a B.S. in psychology from Empire State College. I took
graduate courses in psychology at Syracuse University. I kept
very busy.

All through the years of the war and since, I had been

rushing, speeding, my heart always pounding. I was always struggling against the wind; there was always something I had to fight and overcome. Life was a battle. And then suddenly, or perhaps gradually, my heartbeat slowed down. I didn't have to fight all the elements anymore. I was alive! I was free! I could feel; I had arrived. That was one part of me. There was another part, however, that pulled me, that wouldn't let go, that couldn't forget. Somehow, I had to deal with the past.

One day, I found a way. I sat down at a typewriter and began to write. As soon as I found a free moment, I would rush to the typewriter and pour out my heart. I wrote about everything that had happened to me and my sisters from the day the war started in September 1939 until it ended in May 1945. It all came flooding out, as if a dam had been burst. I had to tell the story, I had to get it out. I wrote to purge myself, but also for the benefit of others. I wrote for the children, for future generations, so they would know what had happened, what could happen in the twentieth century, in a "cultured, civilized" country in the middle of Europe, with the whole world watching and doing nothing. If it happened there, why couldn't it happen here, anywhere?

I began teaching about the Holocaust at Syracuse University, at high schools, at churches and synagogues, anywhere I could find an audience. This became my life's work, to tell this story in the hope that I can play a part in ensuring that it will not repeat itself. When Henry retired in 1980, we moved to Florida, and I continued teaching in the public schools and universities of South Florida. I was invited to serve on the Florida State Board of Education, training teachers to teach about the Holocaust, and speaking in schools as a survivor.

Henry and I enjoyed his retirement, playing golf together and taking courses at the university. One day in 1987, after a quiet evening together listening to music, Henry began to moan and groan, fighting for breath. This had happened a few times before, but this time it looked more serious. I helped him to get dressed and practically carried him to the car. I drove as fast as I could to the emergency room. I stood at the desk filling out forms, asking questions, while through a glass door I could see doctors standing over him, nurses giving him needles, placing a mask over his mouth, moving, rushing, talking. My head was spinning, my stomach aching. I paced the floor. The waiting was endless.

I must have fallen asleep, for the nurse touched my shoulder and I jumped. "It's OK," she said, "He is going to the third floor, room 306; you may come with him." I followed her to the elevator as his bed was wheeled in. He had so many machines around him but I was able to take his hand. We spent two weeks in room 306. I went back and forth three, four times a day. When I was home I ached to be with him, and when I sat at his hospital bed I couldn't wait to leave and go home.

The two weeks finally passed and the doctors sent him home. He had to use oxygen, and couldn't leave the house without an oxygen tank. Most of the time he just stayed home and did nothing. I suddenly found myself a prisoner in my own home. I was afraid to leave him alone. During the night, I would hear him tossing and turning. Many a night, he would wake me up and say: "I don't want to live any longer; I can't go on like this. I can't breathe. I have to fight for every breath. I want to die." Sometimes I was mad at him for doing this to me. I was mad at the whole world, and I was mad at God. This was the last straw, I thought. I have suffered the agony of the Holocaust, the loss of my parents and brother, the death of my beautiful Ellen at the tender age of four. Somehow, I had it in my mind that enough was enough. Hadn't I paid my dues?

One quiet evening I decided to have a talk with Henry. I couldn't and wouldn't let the rest of our lives slide by. I couldn't let his illness ruin what time we had left together. After all, there were still days when he could function. I encouraged him to get out of the house more, to play a few holes of golf when he could, to take a short walk with me, or just to talk with me, enjoying our time together instead of always focusing on his illness. He pulled me close and kissed me, promising to make an effort. That night I woke up and saw him sleeping and breathing peacefully next to me. A wonderful feeling of peace and gratitude enveloped my whole body. Instead of resentment and pity, I felt love. We had lived through other things together; we would conquer this, too.

Henry did try to engage himself in life more after that. We got out and spent time with people. We spent the summer of 1988 in New Hampshire, and he felt good. We were back home for High Holidays, and we went to temple together and prayed like never before. I could see that Henry believed in God, and the prayers gave him peace. We spent Thanksgiving night with my sisters and uncles and aunts. It was really a day to be thankful for. We gave thanks to God for all we had, for helping us to survive hell and for bringing us to a time and a place where we could enjoy life. We also prayed for the parents, sisters, brothers, and other family members we had lost those many years ago, but Thanksgiving day was a celebration of life for all of us.

That Thanksgiving night, when we got home, Henry was getting ready for bed when suddenly he called to me. I rushed to his side. He was struggling to breathe. He put his head on my shoulder and then he slipped to the floor. I screamed. I touched his face; I could see that he was not breathing. I dialed 911. The ambulance came within minutes, but it was too late. He was dead.

Our children, family, and friends all came for the funeral. Our dear friend Rabbi Lipman, who had liberated us from the war, and who had helped us bury our dear daughter, came from Washington to conduct Henry's funeral. Once more I had to turn to God for the strength to overcome another tragedy. I had to reach for my survival skills to help me go on living. It helped a lot that I could turn to my sisters, who had all settled in Florida themselves, and were nearby. My life has been and always will be shared with the lives of my sisters; we have seen each other through more losses than most people know in a lifetime. We all still live quite close to each other and spend a lot of time together.

Pola and Dolek built a happy life for themselves and their twin boys. Dolek worked very hard, built a great business, and gave his children the best education anyone could hope for. Both boys became prominent physicians, and have two wonderful children each. Fifteen years after they arrived in the States, Pola was blessed with another brilliant boy, and I'm his godmother. He is married and lives in New York. I believe that Pola has reached a time in her life when the past doesn't overwhelm her anymore. She is very happy and enjoys life fully.

My youngest sister Anna, the one with whom I share the closest bond, had a very difficult time coming to grips with the horrible experiences of her childhood. The lasting health effects made it very difficult for her to become pregnant, but after years of trying, she finally gave birth to a wonderful son in 1953. Her life changed then, and she was able to emerge from the nightmares. Finally she began to feel free. I don't believe Anna has ever fully recovered from the physical and psychological trauma she suffered as a child in the ghettos and concentration camps, but she enjoys life and tries to grab all she can. She and her husband live a happy life, and enjoy their wonderful son, Ricky. He now lives in Indonesia with his wife and daughter, and works for an oil company.

Mania and Sam started out in Providence, Rhode Island, with their baby daughter, but soon moved to the Bronx, where Sam started a business and made a good living. They had another daughter, and the two of them are now married with three children apiece. Mania and Sam retired to Florida ten years ago. Unfortunately, Mania is sick with Alzheimer's disease; Sam takes wonderful care of her. We live only about thirty minutes away from each other. The children come to visit and I see them quite often.

Gienia, my adopted sister and my aunt, has also moved to Florida. Sadly, my uncle Jack died in 1984. Gienia and I still see each other regularly. She is president of a survivors' group in the town where she lives. One of my father's sisters, Cyla, and a brother, Uncle Aziu, also survived; I see them often and we are close.

My very dear friend Rabbi Eugene Lipman became the rabbi at Temple Sinai in Washington, D.C. He served as president of the Central Conference of American Rabbis (the governing body of Reform Judaism), and he and his wife Esther, a very hard-working psychiatric social worker, have continued to help people and have touched many lives. He was certainly a steadfast friend to me and my whole family. He liberated us from the war; he married Henry and me, and also performed the marriage ceremonies for all of my sisters and all our children; he buried my Ellen, and my beloved Henry. He was there throughout all our lives to lend his support and encouragement. Rabbi Lipman died in February 1994. We all miss him terribly.

Life goes on now, and I continue to be very busy teaching and lecturing about the Holocaust and serving on the Florida State Board of Education. I keep in close contact with all my sisters, and I enjoy visits with my wonderful children. Vivian Ann, a warm, sensitive human being, is married to a brilliant cardiologist. Jeffrey Dan is also a talented physician, and is married to a lovely young lady. I now have three precious grandchildren, who keep me alive and happy.

I have lived through many horrible things, but I am content with my life. Above all, I treasure life's most precious gift: freedom. The road to freedom has been very long and very hard. The physical difficulties were of course staggering, but not less so the psychological adjustments to freedom. I hope that one day the whole world will comprehend the real meaning of freedom. In the meantime, I continue to work and to hope.